PSL MODEL RAILWAY GUIDE

2
Layout Planning

Michael Andress

 Patrick Stephens, Cambridge

First published in 1979

British Library Cataloguing in Publication Data

Andress, Michael
  Model railway guide.
  2: Layout planning
  1. Railroads — Models
  I. Title
  625.1'9   TF197

  ISBN 0 85059 359 X (softbound)

Cover photograph by Brian Monaghan, taken at the Wakefield Model Railway Society.

Text photoset in 8 on 9pt Univers by Stevenage Printing Limited, Stevenage. Printed in Great Britain on 90 gsm Pedigree coated cartridge and bound by The Garden City Press, Letchworth, for the publishers Patrick Stephens Limited, Bar Hill, Cambridge, CB3 8EL, England.

Contents

Introduction

Railway modelling is a very popular pastime with more enthusiasts taking up the hobby every year. Many of the newcomers start with a train set and the transition from this to a more permanent model railway layout is an important step for them. The scope of railway modelling is very wide indeed, ranging from the miniature engineering involved in constructing model locomotives, through the applications of electrical and electronic circuitry in model railway control, to the artistic aspects of structure and scenery modelling. The many different interests brought together in the hobby lead to great variety in the types of layouts built. This is one of the attractions of the hobby but the great choice can also be bewildering to the beginner who does not yet know where his special interests and skills may lie.

Railway modelling is also different from most other constructional hobbies in that we do not only model locomotives or trains just to be displayed as static items, or to be operated as individual models. Instead, our model represents a working railway complete with its surrounding landscape. This adds greatly to the interest. It also means that even though a layout may be complete enough for enjoyable running, construction can continue with the addition of extra models and details, and perhaps by extending the layout. The modeller can thus alternate construction and operation as he pleases, maintaining the interest and enthusiasm. In this way some layouts have been built up over many years and are now very large and elaborate. There is a danger that the beginner, when he sees pictures of these, may be tempted to tackle something too ambitious.

For the construction of a model railway layout which will continue to provide pleasure for the owner, some advance planning is necessary. It is also important to have some idea of what sort of layout is wanted. Often the beginner does not have the knowledge or experience to decide. My aim in this book is to give him some idea of the possibilities and to provide advice on the type of layout he can successfully tackle as a first project.

The term layout planning can be used in a rather restricted sense to describe the designing of the actual track arrangement, the number and positions of the platforms and other details. However, there is a great deal more than this for the modeller to consider in his planning and I want to use the term in a much wider context. We must decide on the size, shape, location and type of model railway layout and even the sort of structures and scenery which will be added. These, and other aspects, are all of importance in the creation of a satisfying model railway layout.

The book covers planning for 00-scale and N-scale layouts of types suitable for beginners. These are the most popular scales in this country, particularly 00, and are the ones best suited to the inexperienced modeller.

The ideas and information presented here are based on the experiences of many modellers. Over the years there have been many interesting developments in layout planning, particularly with regard to small layouts suitable for modern houses. Because an idea devised by one modeller is often modified and improved by others it is difficult to know how any particular scheme first originated. I would, however, like to give credit to the work of Cyril Freezer, now editor of *Model Railways* magazine, who has designed many interesting small layouts and who has done much to popularise the concept of branch line modelling.

I would like to thank all those modellers who have kindly allowed me to use photographs of their work to illustrate this book. In particular I am grateful to Graham Bailey, Tony Butler, Leo Campbell, K.J. Churms, Howard Coulson, Brian Dorman, Keith Gowen, David Hammersley, Dave Howsam, Terry Jenkins, Bob Jones, Ron Prattley, Phil Savage, Mike Sharman, Allan Sibley and Adrian Swain.

Some general considerations

Because we are modelling a whole system rather than just a few separate items which could be displayed on shelves or in a cabinet we must find space to accommodate our layout. To complete a model railway there are many models to be constructed or purchased and time and money will be required. Thus when deciding what sort of layout to build we must take into account the amount of space, time and money we can afford and also how long a period we are prepared to let the construction of the layout take. Obviously there is no point in planning a large and complex system if there is space for only a very small layout. What is often less evident to the beginner is the heavy commitment in hours of work and in cost involved in the building of a large model railway. Many

The Isle of Purbeck MRC 4 mm scale Swanage Branch layout was modelled very closely on the prototype line and is very realistic. However most modellers do not have the space or time to construct such a large layout and must compress and compromise much more.

Some general considerations

Part of the attractive DJH Models 00-scale demonstration layout which was constructed entirely from commercially available items. Note how the small factory utilises the space in the corner of the layout providing not only scenic interest but also a siding to add to the operating scope of the line.

really big layouts have been built over many years by modellers who have been able and willing to devote a great deal of time and money to the hobby. It is essential not to be too ambitious in the choice of a first layout. Later, if the modeller finds he can spare more space, time and money he can tackle a more extensive project.

The track design is very important in determining the appearance of a model railway and how it can be run so it should be planned with some care. However, do not worry too much about trying to make your plan perfect; it never will be! Your first layout is most unlikely to be your final one and, indeed, will probably be very different from what you eventually decide you want in a layout. As you gain knowledge and experience you will want to modify, improve, alter and extend your layout and later you will probably decide to scrap or sell it and build a new and better one, incorporating those features you have come to realise you want to include. So, while it is wise to give some thought to planning your model railway before starting construction, do not spend too long 'armchair modelling'—planning, designing and dreaming without actually building anything! There is no substitute for practical experience.

Though track planning will be discussed later in this book I would suggest that the beginner may well do best to choose a published plan, the basic design of which appeals to him, and to modify it as necessary to suit his own tastes, rather than try to make up his own plan. Small changes will give individuality to the published plan without affecting the essential features. In this way problems of design, some of which may only become apparent too late in construction for easy correction, will be avoided. Do not feel that you are showing a lack of originality by copying a plan in this way. There is only a limited number of workable schemes suitable for small layouts and most, if not all, of these must already have been utilised. Many track plans have been published in the model railway magazines, particularly in *Railway Modeller*, and Cyril Freezer has collected many of his layout plans into three books of which *60 Plans for Small Railways* is especially useful to the beginner.

When we plan a model railway we should always remember that the function of the prototype, with the exception now, perhaps, of the preserved lines, is to provide transportation. On some railways this is very specialised, for example, commuter lines carrying only passengers, mining railways transporting only ore; on others the traffic is mixed, with passengers, both long distance and local, and a wide variety of freight. If a model railway is to be realistic and interesting it should seem to be a replica of the real thing not only in appearance but also in operation. We can add variety to the running of the layout and to the rolling stock required by the provision of lineside industries, each with a siding or sidings to be shunted. There is an almost unlimited choice of possible industries, some of which require special types of rolling stock to serve them, and this is another way in which individuality can be introduced into your model railway.

The restrictions of space, time and money obviously limit what can be included on a layout. We have the choice of representing much of the prototype in outline only or of concentrating on a particular part and modelling it in much greater detail. Interesting layouts of both types have been built but model railways which specialise in an aspect in which the constructor is especially interested are usually more successful than those in which an attempt has been made to include almost everything. However, do remember that railway modelling is a hobby for your pleasure and enjoyment. Plan and build your layout the way you would like to have it and not how others tell you it ought to be. There are so many different aims, interests and ideas among railway modellers that the type of layout other enthusiasts like may not suit you at all. Your model railway is your own private little kingdom where you can express your own ideas and creativity,

and where you can make your own rules. Some enthusiasts will say that you must do this or that on your model because it is prototype practice to do so, but this is not necessarily a valid argument because we can never copy the real thing exactly anyway. Selection and compression are always needed and it is up to the individual to select the parts that he likes and which to him represent the best aspects of the prototype. Provided your layout gives you enjoyment and satisfaction it is a success!

The train set

The train set is the traditional introduction to railway modelling and it remains an excellent way of starting the hobby. The basic set usually consists of a locomotive, coaches or goods stock, and an oval of sectional track about 3½ ft × 2½ ft. Many different sets are produced with various combinations of steam, diesel or electric outline locomotive and coaches or goods vehicles. Some sets include additional track and one or more turnouts for sidings or a passing loop. Nowadays the models are generally of very good quality, they are accurate and well detailed and make an excellent basis from which to develop your layout. If the set is a gift the choice will already have been made for you, but if you are buying the train set yourself try to select a set which will not only meet your present needs but which will also

This simple first permanent layout was developed easily and quickly from a train set.

8

be appropriate for your future layout. Your interests may change or become more specialised but it is obviously helpful if you have some idea of how you might want your railway to develop; if it is to follow British, American or European prototype, if it will be period steam or modern image diesel and so on. This may help to avoid the need for the replacement of locomotives and rolling stock at a later date.

Although it may be tempting to select a large and impressive express locomotive with main line coaches, a better choice is a small steam or diesel engine with a train of goods stock. A large locomotive will look out of place on a small layout with sharp curves, whereas a small engine will be equally at home on the train set oval or on the larger and more complex layout which you may build up from it eventually. I suggest goods vehicles as the initial items of rolling stock because they provide more opportunities for shunting when you add a few sidings. When you later acquire passenger stock, select short branch line coaches rather than full length main line stock. They will look better on sharp curves

and will allow you to use shorter platforms with a consequent saving in space.

Although the simple oval is convenient it has very limited operational scope. You can run a train clockwise or anti-clockwise around the track and that is all! While the oval is a useful basis for a small layout, providing as it does a continuous run in a small area, it needs additional features to make it more interesting. Even a single siding will permit us to drop off and pick up wagons. A run-around loop will give greater scope for shunting because the siding can then be worked by a train running in either direction. Further sidings provide additional permutations for shunting and extra interest. For example, we can represent a small industrial line with, perhaps, three sidings, each serving a factory or warehouse, and this will give considerable operating potential. As the track is sectional you can try out various

Eastern Models feature a timber works on their HO-scale demonstration layout. This industry is served by two sidings giving extra scope for shunting.

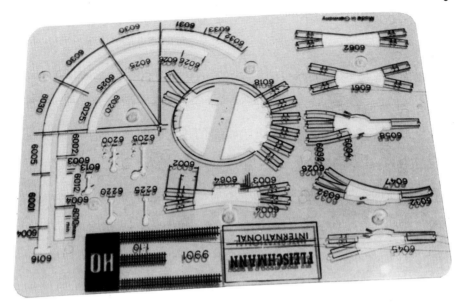

arrangements as you buy extra track and points. This can be a very valuable period of experimentation. There are many different ways of setting out the track and these will produce a variety of operating patterns. Running trains over these different track layouts may give you some idea of the sort of permanent layout you would like to build. You may, perhaps, enjoy watching the trains run steadily on a continuous line or you may prefer the challenge of shunting on a small, but complicated, industrial layout.

It is best to add gradually to the train set rather than to buy a lot of additional parts all at once. In this way you can experiment to the full with the track you have as you go along and you will have more idea of which extra pieces you would find most useful. Similarly with additional locomotives and rolling stock it is preferable to build up gradually from the basic set, so that you can, if you wish, change your mind about the type of railway you want without having to dispose of a lot of equipment, previously acquired but now unsuitable.

For a permanent model railway layout using flexible track a track plan is required as a guide, but it is more difficult to draw out a small scale plan for a layout using sectional track because it must be very accurate or the fixed pieces of sectional track may not fit

The Fleischmann HO-track stencil allows accurate planning to 1:10 scale of layouts with Fleischmann track pieces, points, crossings, etc.

when you come to lay the track. The easiest method is to lay it out full size using actual track pieces to make sure of the positioning. However, you may want to try out various designs on paper without having to buy the track sections until you decide on one particular plan, so that you can then buy just the pieces needed. Some manufacturers produce track stencils to enable the drawing up of accurate small scale plans of layouts which can be built using the sectional track which they make. They include Hornby (00 scale), Arnold (N scale) and Fleischmann (HO and N scales).

The train set has much to recommend it as a starting point for railway modellers. The sets are relatively inexpensive and you can build up from them gradually as your finances permit. The track is easy to assemble and provides good running; being sectional it allows the modeller to try out many different track layouts. The models are realistic and the train set can give a great deal of enjoyment as well as providing useful experience. It can be incorporated into a permanent layout later if you wish.

Some general considerations

Scale and Gauge

Some of the basic terms in railway modelling are often used rather loosely and the beginner may become confused by them. In view of this I feel that it is worthwhile first of all to explain the difference between scale and gauge and the relationship between 00 and HO scales and between Continental and British N scales.

Scale refers to the proportion between the prototype and the model. *Gauge* is the track width, measured between the inner surfaces of the running rails. The British prototype standard gauge is 4 ft 8 ½ in.

For 00 the scale is 4 mm to the foot; that is each foot on the prototype is represented by 4 mm on the model. Alternatively this can be expressed as a ratio of 1:76. The track gauge for 00 is 16.5 mm. HO scale is 3.5 mm to the foot or a ratio of 1:87, also with a track gauge of 16.5 mm. As we have two different scales with the same track gauge, representing in each case the standard 4 ft 8 ½ in gauge prototype, the track gauge must be incorrect for one of the scales. In fact it is in 00 scale that the track width is wrong, being narrower than it should be. This discrepancy arose soon after the commercial introduction of 00 gauge. At first it was intended that the scale should be half 0 scale, making it 3.5 mm to the foot with the virtually correct track gauge of 16.5 mm. However, manufacturers soon found that the small size of the British prototype loading gauge (the maximum permissible height and width for locomotives and rolling stock), compared to those in Europe and the United States, created two problems. The first was the difficulty of fitting the electric motors commercially produced at that time into the British prototype locomotives. The second concerned parts such as axle guards, bogie sides and locomotive valve gear. These parts had to be made thicker than scale to give them enough strength for commercially produced models. It was also necessary to increase clearance in proportion to the prototype to allow models to run on the sharp curves

needed on model railway layouts. The small British loading gauge allowed insufficient width for these increases and so the manufacturers adopted the slightly larger scale of 4 mm to the foot while retaining the 16.5 mm track gauge, the combination being named 00. With the development of smaller scales it is clear that the compromise is no longer necessary but manufacturers and modellers are now so heavily committed to 00 scale that a change to HO scale for British modelling is most unlikely. European and American manufacturers, with the benefits of the larger prototype loading gauges retained 3.5 mm scale and 16.5 mm gauge as HO scale.

00 in Britain and HO in Europe and America have become the most popular of all scales and this is reflected in the vast ranges of ready-to-run equipment, kits of all types, and parts which are produced. These scales are a good compromise in size, being small enough for an interesting layout to be built in a reasonable space, but large enough for good detailing and for relatively easy kit construction and scratch-building. The models are also easy to handle. The convenience of having such a wide variety of products on the market should not be underestimated. It means that a layout can be fairly quickly brought to the stage where it can be operated, whereas progress would be much slower if many of the items had to be hand-built, and the delay might then cause the modeller to lose interest and enthusiasm, particularly if he is a beginner. The proprietary models used to complete the layout initially can be replaced later by more detailed kits or scratch-built items if desired. Another advantage of the availability of good quality commercial products is that the modeller has more time to concentrate on those aspects of the hobby which interest him most. In addition the large potential market for products in 00 and HO scales encourages manufacturers to offer models of less popular prototypes and of more specialised items which in other scales could

not be profitably produced. Thus the modeller has a wider choice. The greater opportunities for mass production also means that the models may be less expensive.

Most modellers of British prototypes are prepared to accept the incorrect scale/gauge ratio of 00 for the convenience and advantages of the large range of commercial items on the market, and so that their models will be compatible with those of their friends. If you find the slightly narrow gauge appearance of 4 mm scale on 16.5 mm gauge unacceptable you can model to EM scale (4 mm scale on 18 mm gauge) or to the exact Protofour standards (4 mm scale on 18.83 mm gauge) but either will involve you in more conversion and construction work than is necessary in 00 scale.

N scale was introduced commercially in the early 1960s by the German firm Arnold, with models to a ratio of 1:160, representing a scale of approximately 1.9 mm to the foot, running on track of 9 mm gauge. Unfortunately, for exactly the same reason that British prototypes were modelled to 00 scale instead of HO, it was considered necessary for the slightly larger scale of 2 $\frac{1}{16}$ mm to the foot, a ratio of 1:148, to be used for commercially produced models of British locomotives and rolling stock, and this has become the standard for British N scale. The track gauge is the same as for Continental and American N scale—9 mm.

N scale is well established and is now second only to 00 and HO scales in popularity. It offers a significant space advantage over the larger scales. A wide variety of models is available and the range of ready-to-run equipment, kits and parts is steadily increasing all the time. N scale has the advantage that standards for track, wheels and couplings were established early on so that all the models produced are compatible in these respects. Thus the modeller does not have the expense or trouble of having to change wheels or couplings to match his own equipment. The present N-scale standards for wheels and track are rather coarse in comparison to those in the larger scales. This makes for reliable running but does detract from the appearance. There have been moves to introduce finer scale standards in N scale and it may be that the manufacturers will adopt these eventually.

I have discussed 00 and N scales in some detail because these are the scales the beginner is most likely to choose; I would certainly recommend that one of these be selected. Of course the choice may already have been made by the gift or purchase of a train set, by the gift of some equipment from a railway modelling friend, or because someone you know has a layout and you want to work to the same scale.

If you have not yet decided I suggest you look at the models in the shops, at exhibitions, or on a friend's layout to see which scale appeals most to you. You might even like to buy one or two kits and make them up to see how you find working in the different scales before you commit yourself too far to want to change. 00 scale has the advantage of being less fiddly to handle and kit construction and scratch-building tend to be easier because of the larger size. Though, conversely, some workers in N scale claim that as less detail is required they find it easier to build models in the smaller scale than in 00. Really it all comes down to your own preferences and to getting used to modelling in any particular scale. The small size of N scale may make it possible for you to fit a more interesting layout into the space you have available. The choice is up to you depending on the circumstances and on your personal feelings about the appearance and feel of the models. Do not make the mistake of thinking that it will be cheaper to model in the smaller N scale! The locomotive and rolling stock models tend to be fairly similar in price in 00 and N scales for comparable quality because the expense of manufacture is much the same. In fact an N-scale layout may well cost you more because you can fit so much more into the same space than on an 00-scale model railway.

Definitions

As I have already indicated I feel that the beginner should start with 00 or N scale. The following brief listing of scales and gauges is provided for general interest and information and so that you will be familiar with them when you see them mentioned in model railway magazines, rather than because I am suggesting other alternative scales for the beginner. Later, after experience in 00 or N scale, the modeller may wish to try out another scale and by then he will be in a better position to assess what this will involve.

Z scale (1.4 mm to the foot or 1:220; 6.5 mm gauge; prototype gauge equivalent 4 ft 8¼ in).

This is the most recently introduced commercial scale. The models, by Märklin, are remarkably well detailed but are expensive and only Continental prototypes are produced. A few plastic structure kits are made for this scale by Kibri.

N Scale — US and Continental (1.9 mm to the foot or 1:160; 9 mm gauge; prototype gauge equivalent 4 ft 8½ in).

Now well established and second only to HO scale in popularity in America and Europe. There is a wide range of ready-to-run models of high quality with the advantage that wheel and rail standards are generally uniform and that there is a universal coupling, so that stock from different manufacturers can be run together. Many kits and parts are also marketed.

N Scale — British (2⅛ mm to the foot or 1:148; 9 mm gauge; prototype gauge equivalent 4 ft 4½ in).

This is also now very popular being second only to 00 scale in Britain. There is a reasonable selection of ready-to-run locomotives and rolling stock and a steadily increasing range of kits, including a variety of cast metal locomotive body kits to fit onto commercial chassis. Many structures and accessories are now on the market, either ready-made or in kit form. The large range of excellent Continental structure kits can also be utilised, sometimes with minor modifications to make them appear more British. These European kits are strictly speaking slightly underscale for British N-scale layouts but this is not really noticeable in practice and can even be an advantage, particularly in the case of large buildings, as the structures will occupy a little less space than if they were to exact scale.

000 Scale (2 mm to the foot or 1:152; 9.5 mm gauge; prototype gauge equivalent 4 ft 8½ in).

This is a scale for the enthusiast who is prepared to hand-build most of his models himself and it is not suitable for inexperienced workers. There is an active 2 mm Scale Association which provides considerable assistance for modellers working in this scale.

TT Scale — Continental (2.5 mm to the foot or 1:120; 12 mm gauge; prototype gauge equivalent 4 ft 8½ in).

There has been a revival of interest in this scale in Germany recently with the reintroduction of the old East German Zeuke products in revised and improved form as Berliner Bahnen. This firm offers a good range of locomotives and rolling stock and also figures and road vehicles.

TT Scale — British (TT3) (3 mm to the foot or 1:100; 12 mm gauge; prototype gauge equivalent 4 ft).

Though the scale received a setback with the introduction of N scale and no ready-to-run models are at present made, there is still a range of kits and parts available and modellers are supported by an active association, the 3 mm Society, which produces its own magazine *Mixed Traffic* for its members. The scale offers a compromise between 00 and N scales but the lack of ready-to-run equipment makes it unsuitable for the beginner.

HO Scale (3.5 mm to the foot or 1:87; 16.5 mm gauge; prototype gauge equivalent 4 ft 8½ in).

The most popular scale by far in the United States and on the Continent with a very extensive range of ready-to-run equipment, kits, parts and accessories.

00 Scale (4 mm to the foot or 1:76; 16.5 mm gauge; prototype gauge equivalent 4 ft 1½ in).

The most popular scale in Britain with many advantages for the beginner despite the inaccurate scale/gauge ratio.

EM gauge (18 mm gauge with 4 mm to the foot scale; prototype gauge equivalent 4 ft 6 in) gives a much better appearance and track is now available from Ratio, though locomotives and rolling stock must be modified by the modeller. The EM Gauge Society provides assistance for workers in this gauge.

Protofour — P4 (18.83 mm gauge with 4 mm to the foot scale; prototype gauge equivalent 4 ft 8½ in). This is a system with an exact scale/track gauge ratio and also a set of fine scale standards for track, wheels and other details. The Protofour Society provides advice and information and a number of items are now commercially available for the system. The results are excellent but the beginner should acquire experience with 00 scale first.

S Scale ($\frac{3}{16}$ in to the foot or 1:64; $\frac{7}{8}$ in gauge; prototype gauge equivalent 4 ft 8 in).

There are some commercial items available for this scale in the United States but not in Britain. It is a useful compromise between 00 and 0 scales but is not suitable for the beginner because models must be hand-built.

0 Scale — British (7 mm to the foot or 1:43; 32 mm gauge; prototype gauge equivalent 4 ft 7 in).

An attractive scale because of the size and weight of the models and the detail which can be included, but generally not suitable for the beginner because of the expense involved and the space needed. There are a number of inexpensive locomotives and rolling stock models of Continental manufacture available, some of British prototype, but the range is very limited.

1 Scale (10 mm to the foot or 1:30.5; 45 mm gauge; prototype gauge equivalent 4 ft 6 in).

Even more expensive in space and cost than 0 scale. There is a range of ready-to-run locomotives and rolling stock of Continental prototype from Märklin.

Narrow gauge

Narrow-gauge modelling has become very popular in recent years, partly because of the numerous preserved lines now in operation but mainly due to the introduction of commercial ready-to-run models, kits and parts in some scales. A railway is narrow gauge if its track width is less than the standard 4 ft 8 ½ in, but most modellers tend to choose prototypes of metre gauge or less. Apart from the undoubted charm of these railways there are advantages for the modeller because the sharp curves, steep gradients, small locomotives, short trains and simple stations typical of narrow-gauge lines enable a model to be built in a smaller space than a standard-gauge model railway would need.

If we set out to model a narrow-gauge prototype we can use one of the commercially produced gauges and choose the appropriate scale to go with it or we can decide on the scale we will model to and make the gauge to suit. Generally it is best to employ a recognised gauge so that commercial wheels, mechanisms and, if desired, track can be used. If the scale and gauge are chosen so that the scale is also one which is catered for by the trade we have the ideal arrangement. We can use items such as structures, figures, road vehicles, and other accessories from the scale chosen while employing wheels, mechanisms, bogies and so on from the smaller scale which has the gauge we are using.

The following are the most usual scale/ gauge combinations:

Nn3 (N scale on Z gauge representing 3 ft gauge prototype). I have not heard of any modellers in Britain using this combination so far but a few American enthusiasts have built narrow-gauge layouts in N scale using locomotives and rolling stock converted from Märklin Z-scale models. Unfortunately the high cost of the Z-scale models is likely to deter many modellers but the combination has considerable potential for the modeller who would like an extensive narrow-gauge system in a limited space.

00n2 and HOn2½ (These are respectively 4 mm scale (usually known as 009) and 3.5 mm scale (usually known as HO9 or HOe) on 9 mm gauge track). Strictly speaking the former is equivalent to 2 ft 3 in gauge prototype and the latter approximately 2 ft 6 in but both are used to model prototypes of from 2 ft to 2 ft 6 in gauge. Some ready-to-run models of Continental prototype are available and a variety of British kits are produced including cast metal locomotive body kits to fit onto N-gauge commercial chassis. The modeller can also utilise N-scale locomotive mechanisms, wagon underframes and wheels, coach bogies and so on for his own models. 009 track and points are made by Peco, or N-scale track can be used if the sleepers, which are wrongly spaced, are largely hidden by the ballast. The latter choice enables the modeller to benefit from the more extensive range of points, crossings and other special track available in N scale. Lilliput make a useful dual-gauge (16.5 mm and 9 mm) crossing for 00- or HO-scale layouts which have both standard- and narrow-gauge track.

HOn3 (This is 3.5 mm scale on 10.5 mm gauge track for 3 ft gauge prototypes). It is popular in the United States where brass ready-to-run locomotives and rolling stock, numerous parts and a variety of rolling stock kits are on sale. Ready-made track is also produced. Some of these items are available in Britain from specialist model railway shops.

00n3 (4 mm scale on 12 mm gauge representing 3 ft gauge prototype). Gem in Britain market a number of metal kits for the Isle of Man Railway equipment and TT3 mechanisms and other parts can be used also.

HOm (3.5 mm scale on 12 mm gauge track for metre gauge prototypes). This scale/ gauge combination was formerly catered for by Zeuke of East Germany but ready-to-run locomotives and rolling stock together with sectional and flexible track and points are now produced by Bemo.

0n2¼ (7 mm scale on 16.5 mm gauge track; equivalent to approximately 2 ft 4 in gauge prototype but used to represent gauges of 2 ft 3 in and 2 ft 6 in also). This is an attractive combination as the models are large enough to allow considerable detailing but a layout can be built in the same space as a comparable one in 00 scale. The vast range of mechanisms, wheels, underframes and track parts intended for 00 and HO can be used for convenience and economy and there is a good selection of accessories such as figures and road vehicles for 0 scale. The

Scale and Gauge

Peco locomotive and rolling stock cast metal kits for this scale/gauge combination should help to make it popular.

On2½ (¼ in to the foot scale on 16.5 mm gauge track). This is the American equivalent of the above and has similar advantages.

10 mm, 14 mm and 16 mm scales on 32 mm gauge track (Representing respectively 3 ft, 2 ft 3 in and 2 ft gauge prototypes). The large size of these models means that they can be very well detailed. Some modellers have used the inexpensive Triang Big Big Train (0 gauge) locomotives and rolling stock as a basis for models to these scales. The Triang models are no longer produced but they can sometimes be obtained second hand. Some accessories are available in 10 mm scale and others can be adapted from military modelling kits.

G-gauge (14 mm scale on 45 mm gauge track). The LGB range of ready-to-run locomotives and rolling stock is quite

extensive and is being steadily enlarged. The manufacturer also makes sectional track and points to complete the system. The models are mainly of European prototypes but a few American models are also made. The scale/gauge combination is equivalent to metre gauge.

Broad gauge

The broad-gauge prototypes have not become popular for modelling in the way that the narrow-gauge railways have, though a few layouts have been built featuring models of the Irish 5 ft 3 in gauge railways. Mike Sharman has modelled the old Brunel 7 ft gauge very effectively on his superb Victorian period 4 mm scale layout which also includes standard- and narrow-gauge tracks together with some complex mixed gauge trackwork. Mike Sharman also offers a number of cast metal kits commercially for broad-gauge modelling in 4 mm scale.

A layout built by Terry Jenkins. This 00-scale model railway is typical of the sort of layout a beginner can tackle successfully. The structures are mainly modified kits and the scenic work is straightforward but effective.

Layout size

I have already cautioned the beginner not to be tempted, by seeing large and elaborate model railways, into tackling something too ambitious for his first layout. It is also very easy when studying layout plans drawn to a small scale to underestimate the size that these layouts will be when built. When considering a plan it is a good idea to measure out on the floor the dimensions of the layout so that you can visualise more easily how much space it would occupy. Even a 6 ft × 4 ft layout, usually classified as small, will take up quite a lot of a small or medium sized room, and if you need to carry it at all, you will find it surprisingly massive.

The beginner sometimes has the belief that if a small layout will be good then a large one must be even better! This is quite wrong. A model railway does not have to be large and elaborate to be successful. Indeed, the greatest entertainment comes from a layout when it is fully used and as most modellers usually operate single-handed the layout should not be too big.

There are many advantages in building a small layout as your first model railway. As I indicated earlier the three basic limiting factors when constructing a layout are the time, money and space which we are able and willing to afford. For a small layout the initial financial outlay will be low, particularly if the modeller is progressing from a train set and already has much of the equipment he needs. The further costs incurred during construction will also be small and there will be no danger of progress being held up through lack of money.

Because only a limited number of models can be accommodated on a small layout the modeller can afford to make sure they are of a high standard, either by purchasing more expensive models or by taking the time to build well detailed ones himself. In the relatively small area, progress on scenic work will be encouragingly good for only a few evenings of modelling, and there is again time to attend to all the small details which

make a layout more interesting.

A model railway is a working model and if it is to provide the maximum enjoyment for its owner it must work well. Good track and wiring are essential and it is much easier both to construct and to maintain smooth, accurate track and good electrical contact on a small layout than on a large one, simply because there is so much less of it.

Often lack of space limits the size of layout which can be built and the modeller has no alternative but to settle for a small model railway. However, even if a large area is available it is still advisable to start out modestly. If the plan is chosen with some forethought a small simple layout, which can be completed fairly quickly and easily, can later be extended or incorporated into a larger system. If possible select the site for your layout with this in mind. Many excellent layouts have been developed in this way. John Allen's HO scale 'Gorre & Daphetid', one of the finest model railroads ever constructed, started out as a small layout approximately 6½ ft × 3½ ft in size and this original section was retained, with only minor alterations, as part of the eventually very large and complex system.

Alternatively, when the layout has been completed and has provided all the operating entertainment it can, you may decide to scrap it rather than use it as part of a larger layout. It may be that your ideas have changed and that it will be easier to build a completely new layout as you want it rather than to try to alter the old one. The standard of your modelling work may also have improved so that the original section is no longer up to the standard you want. Though the beginner tends to think of his first layout, while he is planning and building it, as his final one, most modellers do construct more than one layout, in many cases several. This is another advantage of starting with a small layout as you will be more likely to scrap it and start again than if you are heavily committed in time and money to a large layout. Scrapping a small layout is not the extravagance it may seem. The original cost of the layout will have been amply repaid in the pleasure and experience you have gained in building and operating it and many of the parts, perhaps even the baseboard, can be saved and re-used. A fresh start may also stimulate your interest and enthusiasm.

For the beginner I would suggest a layout no larger than about 6 ft × 4 ft for a rectangular layout accommodating a continuous run track plan of some type. If possible it is best to have a central operating well in layouts of this sort. Access to all parts of the layout is then much easier, particularly as it will probably be necessary to have one side of the layout against a wall. The model railway also appears much more realistic to operate as the trains look as if they are really going somewhere rather than just round and round. This seems to be because you have to turn to watch the train as it passes behind you instead of being able to see it all the time from one position as you can when you view the layout from one side.

For a long narrow layout for a point-to-point design, perhaps as an L-shape fitting into the corner of a room, a baseboard with arms of up to about 6 or 8 ft long and 1-2 ft wide is the maximum size I would advise for a first layout.

The track plan for whatever type of layout is selected should be fairly simple with relatively few points. This is important because the number of points included on a layout influences considerably the time taken to build and later to maintain the model railway.

Even if you anticipate that the layout will be a permanent fitting in the room there is much to be said for constructing it as a number of units, each preferably no larger than about 4 ft × 2ft, which can be fixed together rigidly but which can be taken apart if necessary for storage or transportation. Obviously for a portable layout some arrangement of this sort will be essential.

I believe it was Cyril Freezer who once wrote that it is easier to build a good small layout than a good large layout. This is a very true statement and one which all beginners would do well to keep in mind!

Layout location

When planning a layout the beginner may well look around the house trying to find a large space for his model railway. I can remember planning a grandiose scheme and then looking for the largest possible site to accommodate it, but fortunately as a

beginner I never got as far as actually trying to build my dream layout! These larger spaces include sites such as the loft, the garage or a garden shed and all of these have been utilised very satisfactorily by many modellers. As an example, Mike Sharman's large mixed gauge period layout is now being built into the owner's loft. However, Mike is an expert modeller with great experience, capable not only of constructing a large layout on which almost everything is hand-built but also of fitting out his loft to house the railway. It is worth mentioning though that his layout began as a much smaller portable section which has since been incorporated into the present system.

Personally, I would not recommend any of the above sites for the beginner. Generally I do not feel it is the right approach at this stage because in an effort to obtain the use of a space which is probably much larger than is required the modeller is accepting some serious disadvantages. For example, it can be very dusty in a garage, making operation troublesome and causing problems in maintenance. Fitting out a loft or erecting a garden shed may involve so much work and cost that the modeller may never actually get round to building the layout which was the real object of the exercise! All these sites are likely to be cold in winter, so you will either end up not using the layout then or providing heating which will add to the expense. On wet nights the idea of going out to a garden shed to run your railway is not very inviting! There is also the danger that, having created a large space exclusively for a model railway, the modeller may be tempted to start on too large a layout. I also feel that it is a pity to isolate yourself from the rest of the family while working on or running your railway.

Now I know there are exceptions to the comments I have made above. A friend of mine who lived in a bungalow had a fully fitted-out loft with easy access already, so he erected his portable layout in the centre of the loft and used the rest to store his kits, tools, books and so on. In this case the loft was really the equivalent of a spare room and my objections about work needed for fitting out and lack of comfort do not apply. However, most of us are not so fortunate and in general I think it is best to try to find a site within the main part of the house. There are many places in most houses where a small layout of the sort a beginner should be tackling can be accommodated. Indeed successful layouts have been built in small flats, bedsitters and even a caravan!

If you are lucky enough to have a spare

room which can be devoted exclusively to your hobby then there is no problem. More frequently, however, the layout must be accommodated in a room which will be used for other purposes also and it must not interfere unduly with these other activities. Often a youngster will want to develop his train set into a permanent continuous-run layout on a baseboard in his bedroom. A rectangular baseboard of this type does occupy a considerable part of the free area of a room even if its size is kept to a minimum. As it will almost certainly need to be pushed back against a wall, a baseboard with a central operating well is the best arrangement so that access to the whole layout is easy. Unfortunately there is a tendency for a layout like this in a bedroom to become untidy. The models themselves get dusty and things may be left on and under the baseboard making cleaning up difficult. A neat solution to the problem is to arrange the baseboard so that it folds up against one wall when the layout is not in use, leaving the room clear. The layout should be hinged along one edge onto a strong frame fixed firmly to the wall. Shelves or cupboards can be built into the lower part of the frame below the layout to store the locomotives and rolling stock between operating sessions. Hinging the layout in this way does involve additional construction work but it may mean that a layout can be built in a room where it would not otherwise be acceptable. It also ensures that the layout is kept tidy, because

loose models, tools and so on, must be removed before the baseboard is folded up. There will also be more protection from dust and accidental damage for the layout.

An alternative way of installing a permanent layout in a room is to fit a long, narrow baseboard along one or more walls. The most suitable arrangement for the beginner is a layout limited to only one or two of the walls. In this way the door of the room can be left clear avoiding the need for any form of lifting section to be included. This type of layout can conveniently be supported on storage units; many suitable pieces of furniture are available at very reasonable prices from discount stores, either as ready-made units or in kit form for home assembly. If preferred, the baseboard can be fixed to the wall as a shelf. A neat and convenient method is to use one of the slotted shelving systems obtainable from DIY shops. A layout of this type can be fitted into a bedroom with very little effect on the usual purposes of the room. Similarly, if an along-the-wall layout is very neatly finished it may be acceptable in the lounge. If you are really stuck for space do not overlook the possibility of installing a narrow layout along the wall in the hall. In many houses the hall is too small for this but in others there would be ample, otherwise wasted, space.

If you fit a layout into the lounge you may like to have a cover so the layout will be concealed when not in use. This will also protect the model from dust and damage.

A close view of part of a neat 00-scale bookcase layout built by Dave Howsam and Ron Prattley showing the goods yard. Layout is realistic and interesting even though actual width available is only 10½ in. (Photo by Ron Prattley.)

An interesting 009 narrow-gauge layout built in a coffee table. Design is essentially a dog bone with the loops overlapped. (Model, photo and plan by K.J. Churms.)

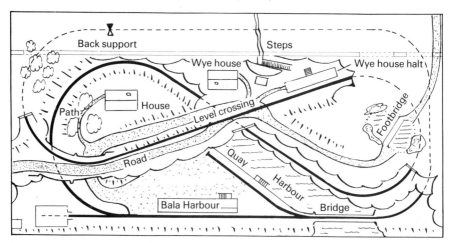

Dave Howsam and Ron Prattley have constructed a very neat bookcase to house a terminus to fiddle yard design model railway. When not in use the model is hidden and the unit looks like a typical bookcase. To set up for operating, the top is removed to reveal the terminus on the fixed part of the bookcase. The top is reversed and fitted onto one end of the unit where it forms the remainder of the layout, including the fiddle yard. The complete layout measures 16 ft in length. The bookcase also provides useful bookshelves and cupboards. An advantage of a unit of this type is that it is free standing and does not require any fixing to the wall as would be needed with a shelf layout. If a more extensive layout is wanted further units can be constructed to carry the railway along a second wall as well. Dave and Ron built their bookcase up from wood and chipboard, but you may well be able to find suitable units, either ready-made or in kit form, which could be adapted for this purpose.

If you do not want to tackle the

An L-shaped portable N-scale layout following German prototype. The model which includes a double-track mainline and a single-track branchline is not yet complete, requiring two further sections at the right-hand end. When not in use the layout breaks down into four sections which can be easily carried and stored.

One of the sections of the German N-scale layout. Three of the units, including this one, measure 40 in × 20 in, the other section is 60 in × 20 in. The modules are bolted together to assemble the layout.

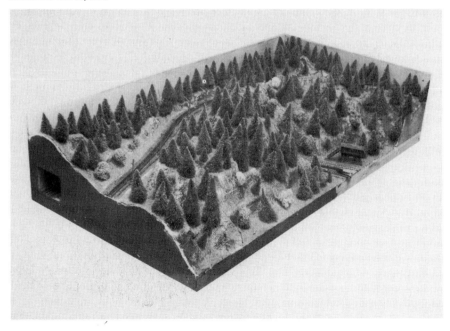

Layout size

construction of a unit as large as a bookcase, but would like a railway layout that can be kept in the lounge, you might consider building a coffee table layout. These very small layouts in 009, N or Z scale usually measure about 3 ft × 1 ½ or 2 ft, and have a continuous run track plan, either an oval or a figure of eight design. The model is built into a coffee table the top, and sometimes also the sides, of which are plate glass. Obviously the scope of such a layout is limited, but nevertheless the construction can provide good experience in everything from track laying to scenic detailing. As can be seen from the layout shown, constructed by K.J. Churms, the finished result can be a very attractive piece of furniture and it will certainly promote interest in railway modelling!

For the modeller with limited space, particularly if his accommodation may not be permanent, a portable layout can be the answer. The layout is made up of a number of sections, each of which should be a maximum of 4 ft × 2 ft, which are set up for operating sessions and stored away afterwards. It is important that they are stored neatly both to keep them out of the way and to avoid damage. Keith Gowen's TT-scale branch line layout is a portable model railway and is stored in a large cupboard when not in use; this is a very convenient scheme and if you have a suitable cupboard it would be worth making your layout sections the correct size to fit into it. An advantage of a portable layout is that construction work can be carried out very conveniently as each section is small and, not being fixed down, can be carried to the workbench or a table. In this way you can work on the model in comfort and under ideal conditions.

The idea of constructing the layout as a series of sections has been taken rather further by some modellers, particularly in the United States. These enthusiasts often build a number of separate units or modules completing each one fully, even to the smallest details, before going on. In some cases the modules offer little or no possibility for operation at the time and are intended more as a convenient way for a modeller without much space to enjoy construction. Eventually if space for a layout becomes available the modeller will have several modules which can be fitted together as the basis of a layout. The module method of building also has some advantages for the beginner in that he can practise construction techniques and enjoy a variety of work on a small unit. Obviously this method does not provide much scope for those interested in operation, though if you can run trains on a club layout or one belonging to a friend you might like to consider it as a way of enjoying construction at home. The modules can be made to a standard size for convenience in building and storage, but need not be the same.

A further step has been taken in the United States with N scale with a system called N-Track. A number of modellers are building standard size modules on which the tracks are arranged so that they are in set positions at the ends of each module. This enables any module to be joined to any other. Standards such as the minimum radius for curves are also set. The system allows units to be linked to form large layouts for exhibitions or for operating sessions when several modellers get together.

Market Redwing station on Keith Gowen's TT-scale portable layout. Neat modelling has resulted in a very realistic appearance. Note the token exchange apparatus in the lower left corner of the picture.

Track schemes

There are only a few basic track designs and all layouts employ one or more of these. The best known, from its train set origin is the oval. It is a very useful arrangement but its appearance must be disguised if it is to be realistic. Concealing part of the oval with scenery is desirable. Part of the toy-like look of the train set oval is due to its symmetry and distorting the oval will help to disguise its nature. Positioning the tracks so that they are not parallel with the edge of the baseboard will also improve the appearance. Often straight track can be replaced by a gently curving line, again showing greater realism. The layout will also look much more realistic if viewed from within the oval by providing a central operating well. The oval gives a continuous run on which the train can travel as long as you wish without the need to stop, turn or reverse and this can be very convenient, especially if you just enjoy watching your models run.

The figure of eight layout provides a greater length of run per lap in the same area as an oval. However it either involves a track crossing at the same level, a feature more typical of US prototypes than on British lines, or at different levels. For a realistic figure of eight layout the scenery must be planned to justify the track arrangements and gradients. This is best done with hills, rivers and other natural obstacles.

The oval—the simplest continuous run design, derived from the train set.

The figure of eight design with tracks crossing on different levels.

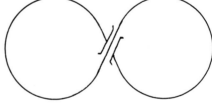

The one level figure of eight design with track crossing provides more length of run per lap than the oval.

The twice around track plan which provides almost double the length of run of the oval in the same area.

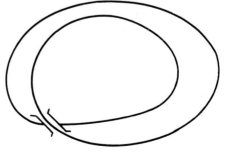

Track schemes

If the design is twisted further a twice around, continuous run plan results. This is a very useful arrangement as it gives about twice the length of run per lap of a simple oval, but again the scenery must be designed to make the track design appear plausible. With a plan of this type it is best to avoid having too much exactly parallel track as this will make the layout less realistic.

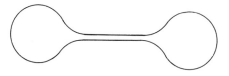

The dog bone is a variant of the oval.

Another form of continuous run scheme is the dog bone, essentially an oval with the sides brought closer together. It can be extended and twisted on itself to give a much longer run. As the two sides of the dog bone can be brought together to resemble double track this design can be used for a main line layout. The loops are the least realistic parts and are best concealed; it may be possible to place one above the other and hide them both together thus saving space on the layout.

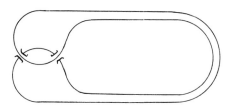

The folded dog bone provides greater length of run. Positioning one loop above the other, either partly as here or completely, saves space.

An entirely different arrangement is the point-to-point track plan. Whereas the oval is derived from the train set, this scheme is based on the prototype resulting in realism and authenticity. The only major disadvantage of the point-to-point layout is that the length of run for the train is limited. The usual design for this kind of layout is a long, narrow one, often running along one or more walls of a room. However, a point-to-point layout design can be twisted on itself into a spiral to

The point-to-point scheme, here as a straight design is often bent into an L-shape to fit into the corner of a room extending along two walls, and can also be bent further into a U-shape to fit onto a rectangular baseboard.

fit onto an ordinary rectangular baseboard. One terminus on a point-to-point layout may take the form of a fiddle yard.

A variant is the out and back scheme in which one terminus (or the fiddle yard in a terminus to fiddle yard design) is replaced by a loop so that the train is brought back to the terminus from which it started. This is a useful arrangement, particularly if the loop is combined with an oval so that the train can

A variant on the point-to-point scheme is the out and back design where the fiddle yard, or one terminus, is replaced by a reversing loop. This design can also be twisted to fit onto a rectangular baseboard.

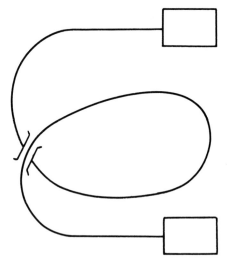

Further twisting results in a spiral point-to-point design giving greater length of run.

make as many laps around the oval as desired before coming back to the terminus. It does, however, require a special wiring arrangement for the reversing loop part of the system. An out and back design can be built on a long, narrow board—though a wider part will be needed to accommodate the loop. Alternatively, the track plan can be twisted into a spiral or figure of eight shape to fit on a shorter, wider rectangular baseboard. A more elaborate reversing loop with extra tracks acting as hidden sidings will make for more interesting operation by allowing the order in which the trains return to the terminus to be varied from that in which they left it.

The Z-shape, zig-zag, or switch-back track arrangement.

An entirely different concept in track planning is the Z-shaped or switchback arrangement. Here a greater length of run for the trains is achieved by having three tracks form a Z-shape, each track being nearly the full length of the baseboard. In fact even more than three tracks can be included if desired. On such a layout the train travels three times the length of the layout (if three tracks are used) and the interest of operation is further increased by the reversing that is needed. Obviously, for the sake of reality we must introduce a good reason for the presence of three parallel tracks. On a small industrial layout the excuse may be that the track arrangement is needed to provide access to all the various factories, warehouses and other industries. Another way in which the scheme can be justified is to provide vertical separation between the tracks. For example on a mining layout a switchback track arrangement can be employed to bring the railway down the hillside in a situation where we can claim that it would have been too difficult or expensive for the prototype to have built curves to bring the line down in one continuous run. The scenery on such a layout must be rugged enough to support this argument. Though the beginner is perhaps best advised to build a single level layout for his first attempt, the switchback design on different levels has some interesting features and is worthy of consideration if lack of space forces you to build a narrow layout. This scheme does not

appear to have been used much in Britain but is more popular in America.

It is of course possible to combine more than one of the basic track arrangements in one layout. For example, a continuous oval plan with a branch leading to a terminus combines the oval and point-to-point types.

Your choice of basic scheme will be influenced by your interests. If you enjoy watching your trains run in a realistic landscape, pick a simple continuous design—do not put in too much track and hide some of the track you have in tunnels and behind hills. If you are more interested in shunting then a point-to-point, or a Z-shaped design with lineside industries to shunt, will probably appeal more.

Basic concepts—Fiddle yards

The idea of the fiddle yard is one which has largely developed with the concept of the branch line point-to-point model railway layout. In the restricted space often available for this type of railway, rather than have two limited terminal stations unrealistically close together it was felt better to concentrate on constructing one rather more interesting terminus. The other end of the line was then led to some hidden sidings which represented the rest of the railway system. At first these sidings were provided with a run around arrangement and were operated much as a normal station would be. Sometimes a turntable was included to allow the engine to be reversed. However, as the sidings were hidden from view anyway, modellers soon found it quicker and more convenient to ignore prototype practice and to provide merely a bank of storage sidings on which the locomotives and rolling stock were rearranged by hand. Hence the name 'fiddle yard'. This is a most useful device as it allows reversal and rearrangement of the trains easily and quickly while using a minimum of space. In fact the yard can often be made detachable so that it is fitted onto the layout during operating sessions only. In this way it increases the rolling stock capacity of the railway and makes operation more interesting. An alternative arrangement to a bank of sidings fed by points is the provision of a traverser table with a single track lead. The table is moved to give access to its sidings. Such a traverser need not be elaborate, but merely a simple sliding board moved by hand, with spring brass contacts for electrical supply to the tracks.

Finding that the rearrangement of trains in the fiddle yard was a rather uninteresting chore for one operator on his well known

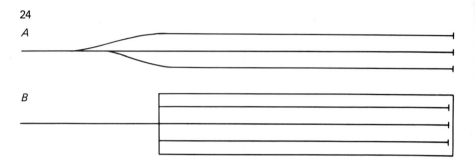

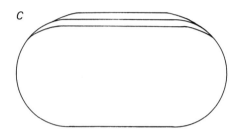

Fiddle yards. Typical fiddle yard (a). A traverser fiddle yard (b). Fiddle yard on concealed part of oval (c).

'Buckingham Branch' layout, Peter Denny devised an ingenious detachable 5 track fiddle yard. When all the trains have entered the fiddle yard it is detached, turned end for end reversing all the trains at once, and replaced. Small end doors are slid in to prevent any stock falling from the yard during turning. Operation can then immediately continue. This method has the additional bonus that stock can be stored in the fiddle yard when the layout is not in use. Not only is the stock kept safe from damage but the trains are ready for running as soon as the yard is fixed onto the layout. The Rev Denny has since further developed his fiddle yard by arranging for reversal without detaching. With a mechanism based on Meccano parts the yard is designed to move away a short distance to give clearance, and the whole fiddle yard then rotates as a train turntable to reverse it. The yard is then moved in again to meet the layout.

An alternative to a fiddle yard for turning trains is to use a series of reversing loop tracks but this requires much more space.

A most ingenious form of fiddle yard has been devised by an American modeller, in the form of a train ferry. The model ferry is mounted on a wheeled cart, very much like an old wooden tea trolley, which he has constructed to match the height of his layout. The trains are run onto the ferry which then 'sails' by being wheeled away on its cart. The ferry could be double ended so

that it could be wheeled back into place with the trains reversed. Again, a ferry fiddle yard can be used for storage, and there will also be space for storage on the trolley underneath it. Plans for a 4 mm scale train ferry are included in the range of Skinley Blueprints and would enable a modeller to construct a realistic model of a British ferry.

Though fiddle yards and hidden sidings are particularly associated with point-to-point branchline layouts they can also be usefully employed to add operating potential to layouts based on other track patterns. For example, the rear of an oval can be concealed and sidings can be provided here for train holding or for use as a fiddle yard. Similarly on an out and back scheme hidden sidings can be led from the reversing loop.

Extendable layouts

A model railway layout, even a small one, will take some time to build. Indeed, as much of the pleasure of railway modelling is in the construction work we would not want to complete the layout too soon. However, it is nice to be able to alternate building and operating as the mood takes us. Ideally we need a layout which begins small, so that we can get something running on it as soon as possible, but which can be extended in stages thus maintaining its interest. In this way there will be a period of track laying and wiring to reach the next stage, followed by a

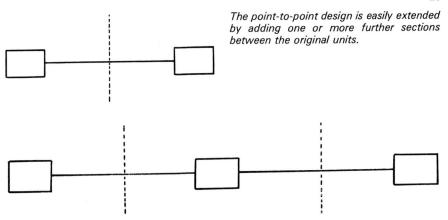

The point-to-point design is easily extended by adding one or more further sections between the original units.

pause to build structures and scenery and perhaps more rolling stock. You can also enjoy operating the extended layout. The layout should be arranged so that it is fully usable at each stage. Thus there will be no need to go on to the next stage until you feel you want to.

The point-to-point type of layout, for example a branch line of the terminus to fiddle yard design, is very easily extended particularly if the terminus and fiddle yard are on separate baseboard sections. All that is needed is to add extra sections between the two original units. At every stage the layout will be fully operational and further sections can be completed at your leisure. Such a system can be very versatile. You can, for example, remove a section you no longer want and replace it with another more interesting one, or you can take one unit out for rebuilding and still run the layout in the meantime. If you want you can even arrange the sections so that they will fit together in more than one order to give extra variety to the operation of the layout. While the additional sections for a point-to-point line will probably be narrow units carrying a single line there is no reason why an oval or spiral should not be included if it suits the space available and you want it.

Many enthusiasts start with an oval track plan, often developed from the train set. The simple oval needs a passing track and a few sidings to make it sufficiently interesting to operate. For the next stage of the layout one of the sidings on the outside of the oval can be extended to form a branch line. This can be carried away from the main oval on an extension of the baseboard or it can be kept on the original base but raised up to a higher level. Alternatively the main oval can be

elevated so that the branch can lead down to a reversing loop beneath it.

Another development of the oval is to raise part of it so that it crosses over the level section to result in a spiral point-to-point scheme. There are many possible ways in which the simple oval can be added to and modified particularly if the so called 'cookie cutter' method of baseboard construction is employed. In this system a simple grid frame is used to support a baseboard top of plywood which is fixed on to the frame with screws only. The tracks are then laid and the railway is used until the modeller wants to develop it further. To raise the level of a track saw cuts are made with a keyhole or sabre saw along each side of the track, taking care not to cut the frame beneath the plywood. Any screws holding this strip down are removed and, the strip and the track it supports, are elevated to the required height. Wooden riser blocks are fitted to hold it in its new position.

It is helpful when planning to extend a layout in this way if you have some idea at the beginning how you will want to do this later. You can then put sidings on the original layout at points where branch lines or other tracks will leave the oval later. Thus the points needed will already be in place avoiding the job of taking up part of the track and fitting points in later.

One of the benefits in building up your layout in stages is that you do not need to decide on the details of these later stages until you actually start work on them. Thus the experience you gain from the first part of the layout will influence the form which the extensions will take, and the finished layout will be more likely to meet your eventual requirements.

Track schemes

The oval can be developed by adding branches inside or outside.

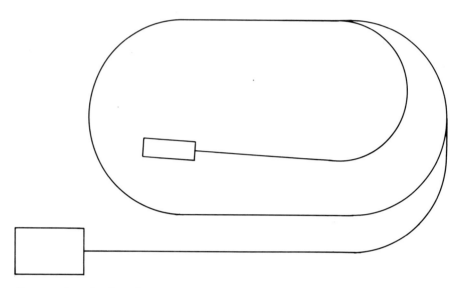

Here two branches have been added but the design is not a good one as a train proceeding from one terminus must reverse, at some stage after reaching the oval, to get onto the other branch.

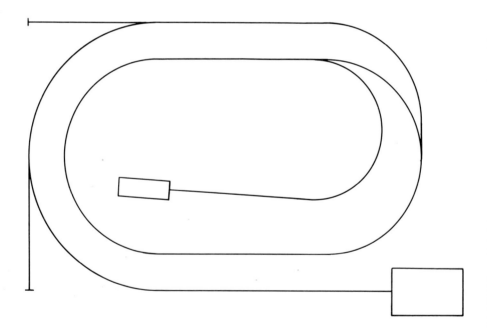

This is the better design and allows interesting operation combining, as it does, a continuous run on the oval with point-to-point operation on the branches.

Model Railway Guide 2

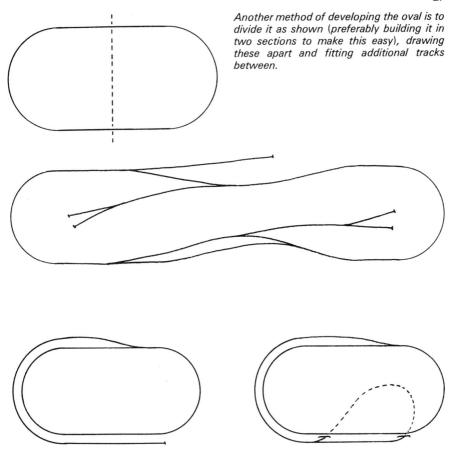

Another method of developing the oval is to divide it as shown (preferably building it in two sections to make this easy), drawing these apart and fitting additional tracks between.

Here the original oval has been elevated so that the branch can go to a reversing loop situated beneath the oval.

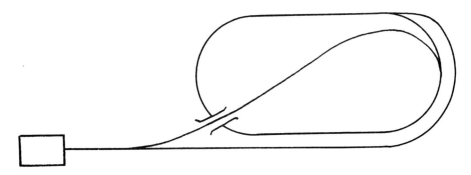

This oval with a single branch has a reversing loop incorporated so that trains can run out and back from the terminus and do as many laps as desired round the oval.

Track schemes

Railway types

On a model railway layout it is quite imposs-ible to include everything and compromise and selection are essential. Obviously it is best to concentrate on the parts of the prototype which interest you most. If your interests are rather varied there is nothing to stop you mixing prototypes and periods on one layout, if you wish, but your model railway is more likely to be satisfying to view and operate if it is more realistic and authentic. The highly accurate and detailed models now available commercially will also look at their best in a proper setting.

Your modelling will benefit from know-ledge of the real thing, either from direct observation of the prototype or from the study of photographs, drawings, railway and model railway magazines and books. Though basing your model on the prototype will help realism it is not generally possible, or even desirable, to try to copy part of a real railway exactly. Instead, select the features which you find the most characteristic and appealing, and leave out those you feel are unnecessary or undesirable, so creating your own ideal representation of the prototype.

There are various types of railways depending on the location, circumstances and type of traffic. We can model our layout on any of these and the following listing gives some idea of the possibilities. There is often some overlap between the different cate-gories; it may also be possible to include more than one type of railway on a layout.

Main line

The main lines with their fast long trains are a very interesting and exciting part of the real railways and there is an excellent selection of suitable model locomotives and rolling stock now available, making a main line a tempting choice. However, to do the prototype justice a large layout with a good length of run, large radius curves, double track and platforms able to accommodate long trains is really desirable. A main line 00-scale layout can be built in a small space but this involves considerable compromise. Train lengths of only 4 or 5 coaches and curves of 18 or even 15 in radius may be required. However, some imagination must be used with any model railway layout, and you may be prepared to stretch it further if you are really set on the idea of a main line layout. A convenient arrangement is a continuous run scheme, either a simple oval or a twice around or figure of eight design so that length of run can be achieved by letting the train make a number of laps of the circuit.

Though I am hesitant to recommend it to the beginner for a first effort, because of its greater extent and the need for a lifting section at the door, a layout around the walls of a room is an ideal arrangement if you are sure you want a main line model. If you have a suitable site and you wish to tackle a layout of this type, start very simply with just a single track circuit. Planning in advance where points will be needed later is helpful as they can then be included in the correct positions in the basic circuit as you lay it. In this way you will avoid the need to remove sections of track later to fit the points in. In due course you can install a second circuit to make the line double track. Station tracks, goods yards, an engine depot, sidings and so on can all be added in stages as time and money are available.

An alternative to the continuous run layout is an L-shaped terminus to fiddle yard scheme of the type developed for branch line models, but with the station adapted for main line practice, though again with restricted train lengths. If the layout is fitted into the corner of a room, it could later be extended, if circumstances permit, by introducing new sections between the station and the fiddle yard. Eventually it could be carried right round the room to form a complete circuit, with the station converted from a terminus into a through type.

In N scale a 180° turn can be made on a 2 ft wide board and this makes it possible to model a main line through station on a

The main station on Graham Bailey's modern period British Rail N-scale layout uses parts from three Pola kits for the glass roof while the remainder of the station was scratch-built.

narrow board along one wall, or curved to fit onto an L-shaped baseboard along two walls, with the baseboard widening to 2 ft at each end to accommodate loops to provide continuous running. The loops can be hidden by scenery to conceal their sharp radii and also the fact that the trains go round and round on the layout. If it is important to keep the layout as narrow as possible throughout, 9 in radius Peco Setrack sectional track can be used for the loops and the turn can be made on a baseboard only 20 in wide.

If the modeller merely enjoys seeing his trains run in a realistic setting, but is not concerned about operation, a very simple diorama type of layout can be constructed in N scale which can be fitted along one wall as a shelf. A dog bone track design will produce what appears to be double track main line while the loops at each end, allowing continuous running, can be concealed. The scenic work should be carried out carefully to give a realistic effect. The landscape can rise at the rear of the layout to cover hidden sidings holding other trains.

Branch line

If we want to achieve a model railway as realistic as possible within the restrictions imposed by a small layout we must look for a suitable prototype and the country branch line in the days of steam is an ideal choice. Trains often consisted of only two or three coaches pulled by a small tank engine and the station track layouts were usually fairly simple. An attractive branch line type of layout can easily be developed from the train set oval and can be an ideal first permanent layout with considerable scope for attractive scenery and structures.

During the 1950s the branch line model railway layout concept was developed considerably. The idea was not so much to provide a suitable subject for beginners as to enable more experienced modellers to create a model railway which would look and operate realistically in a small space. The short prototype trains allowed the modeller to run authentic length trains despite the small size of his layout. Also because the station track layouts are simple on branch lines they can be compressed to fit onto a model railway while still retaining their essential features, so that the model can be operated according to prototype practice and following a proper timetable. Rather than copy any particular station exactly, the modeller will usually do better to select desirable features from various prototypes to produce an interesting and attractive station.

Railway types

Because the aim was realistic operation, the point-to-point track arrangement was preferred to the continuous run schemes and the now classic branch line terminus to fiddle yard (hidden sidings representing the rest of the system) design was developed. Such a track plan can be fitted onto baseboards of various shapes but a popular arrangement is on two narrow baseboards in an L-shape, often fitted into the corner of a room. This

A branch line terminus modelled in 00 scale. The layout is operated as a point-to-point line with a fiddle yard at the other end.

design has the advantage of providing the greatest running possibilities in a minimum area and often a layout of this shape can be fitted into a room whereas a conventional rectangular baseboard would not be accept-

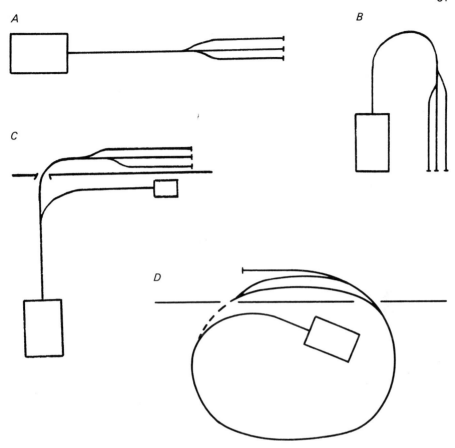

Branch Lines. The basic branch line terminus to fiddle yard design (a). This can be bent to a U-shape if desired (b). An L-shaped terminus to fiddle yard scheme with an additional station, dock, factory or other feature in front of the fiddle yard and separated from it by a backscene (c). The Maurice Deane terminus to fiddle yard design with a backscene separating the two (d). Note the optional link track (dotted) providing a continuous run if required.

able as it would block the centre of the room too much.

A branch line layout of this type is also very suitable for the beginner as it can fairly quickly be brought to a stage where it is interesting to view and operate. However, the scope is limited and in time the modeller will wish to extend the layout. This is another reason for not basing the model accurately on a specific prototype because if you do, once you have completed the model no further development is possible. If, however, your layout is merely based in general terms on the practice of the prototype you have chosen, you are free to alter or add to your model indefinitely.

An interesting alternative to the usual scheme, first employed, I believe, by Maurice Deane, is to fit the branch line on a rectangular baseboard with the fiddle yard behind the terminus but concealed by a low backscene. This has two advantages. The modeller can easily reach both the terminus and the fiddle yard from his operating position in the central well. It also makes it easy to include a link to allow continuous running for locomotives to be run in or when the modeller would like to just sit back and watch the trains in action. The link can be concealed so that the realism of the point-to-point scheme is not impaired.

The branch line provides the opportunity for realistic operation and also has great scenic possibilities. GWR branches are

As the mainline will probably be chosen to model, some compromise will be needed on a small layout but there are some advantages to modern image modelling compared to a mainline layout in steam days. In many cases the trains are now shorter and many tracks have been lifted simplifying track layouts and goods yards. Engine servicing facilities are also much simpler with diesel fuel tanks replacing coal and water and with no need for turntables. The modeller can introduce some modern architecture in addition to the older buildings still in use giving an interesting variety. Overhead catenary is also very effective in model form and a working catenary can be assembled from parts made by Vollmer or Sommerfeldt. In this case two trains can be controlled independently on the same stretch of track, one from the track as usual and one from the overhead.

One of the great advantages of modelling modern railways is that one can still study the real thing easily to gain information on anything from locomotives down to small details such as signs and noticeboards. On the goods side a Freightliner depot would make an interesting working model. As modern trains are often run as block units

The Market Redwing GWR branch layout is a portable one which has been exhibited on several occasions. At shows the railway is operated on an hourly programme and the card system illustrated here indicates to the spectators what the next train movement will be. As each operation is completed the next card is turned down.

particularly popular and are very well catered for with commercial models, but other prototypes can also be followed very satisfactorily if preferred.

Modern image

There is considerable interest in modelling present day British Rail, particularly among younger enthusiasts. The locomotive and rolling stock requirements are generally well catered for by the trade with even the High Speed Train available, as a ready-to-run model in 00 and as a kit in N scale. There is a reasonable range of diesels and a few electrics with further models planned in the ready-to-run category and there is also a selection of diesels and multiple units in kit form, particularly from MTK and Q kits which helps to complete the motive power scene. There is also a good variety of rolling stock suitable for a modern layout.

The attractive Hornby 00-scale model of the British Rail High Speed Train seen on the exhibition layout of the Bournemouth & Isle of Purbeck MRC. Note the non-operating model of a miniature railway on the promenade below the station and the beach at lower right.

Mike Sharman has constructed a fine Victorian period 4 mm scale layout which features standard-, narrow- and broad-gauge track together with some complex multiple gauge trackwork. Careful research and accurate modelling, mostly from scratch, has recreated the atmosphere of the railways of that period very effectively. Locomotive No 10 is a model of Timothy Hackworth's 0-6-0 built in 1838 for the Stockton & Darlington Railway and is the oldest prototype represented on the layout. The working beam engine behind No 10 was also scratch-built.

there is rather less opportunity for train marshalling and shunting on a modern layout, but we can still install some industrial sidings for local shunting.

Period

Though strictly the term refers to any era, including the present, I use it here to mean historical, for any time prior to the contemporary scene. Construction of an historical layout requires research and also care to avoid introducing anachronisms. Depending on the period chosen the modeller may also have to build more or less all his locomotives and rolling stock himself.

The most popular period seems to be the pre-nationalisation era, particularly of the 1930s, and of the four main railway companies, the LMS, the LNER, the SR and the GWR, the greatest following is for the GWR, with especial interest in its branch-lines. There is now a good selection of ready-to-run models and kits enabling the modeller to construct a successful model of this type.

A period which has many advantages but which is not yet particularly popular is the post-nationalisation era of the 1950s. A layout based on this period can mix an interesting variety of steam, diesel and electric locomotives and of rolling stock. The modeller is well served with commercial models and there is no problem in obtaining information and photographs.

At the other end of the time scale are the early Victorian railways. The modeller who chooses these as his prototype will need to carry out considerable research and there is little available commercially to help him in construction. However, if well executed such a layout can be most interesting and attractive. Mike Sharman has built a superb 4 mm scale layout of this period; careful research and skilled scratch-building has created an authentic atmosphere as can be seen in the above photograph.

Going back to even earlier times, 1825-30, the American MRC of Darlington chose the Stockton & Darlington Railway as their prototype and built a fascinating model of great historical interest for the Rail 150 exhibition in 1975. The scale was also 4 mm.

Railway types

A view of W. T. Butler's Dalcross layout, a 4 mm scale model of a 19th century ironworks. The accurate modelling of an unusual prototype and the inclusion of many small, but authentic details, has resulted in a fascinating model. The locomotives, rolling stock, structures and steam lorries were all hand-built.

Industrial

The industrial railway layout has considerable potential in a small space as it can be essentially a shunting layout and need not have an oval or other form of continuous run, though one can be included if desired and if there is sufficient space. In its simplest form the track plan need only have a run-around loop and a number of sidings though the addition of hidden sidings or a fiddle yard,

concealed by structures, low relief buildings or a backscene, will add to the operating potential. For a long, narrow layout the switchback type of track plan is useful for an industrial line, while if a rectangular baseboard can be used an oval with sidings can be a convenient track arrangement.

As the locomotives will be small steam or diesel engines and the rolling stock mainly goods vehicles, the layout can have sharp

There are many prototype industries which can be adapted to make interesting features for model railway layouts. This small scrap yard in 4 mm scale was based on a yard in Newcastle but was considerably compressed to suit the space available on a layout.

curves. If the modeller wishes he can include some interesting trackwork as the prototype is often cramped and needs slips, 3-way or lap points, curved points and crossings. The track is often set into roads or wharves so that road vehicles can cross the tracks easily and this should also be represented on the model.

There is a good selection of suitable small locomotives in ready-to-run and kit form. Centre Models have specialised in industrial steam locomotives, offering cast metal kits for four different types in 00 scale, and some of the smaller engines made by other cast metal kit manufacturers are also ideal for a layout of this type. A wide range of suitable rolling stock both ready-to-run and in kit form is on the market.

The layout can be based on one major industry such as a mine and processing plant, a large factory or a shipyard, or can represent an industrial area or estate with a variety of different types of industries giving scope for a wide range of rolling stock. A dock or canal is often very attractive in model form.

The small size of N scale makes it possible to represent the larger industries more realistically than is usually possible in 00 scale. Graham Bailey modelled this shipbuilding yard for his N-scale British Rail layout using a modified Novo Shell Welder kit as the ship under construction.

An industrial layout also offers excellent opportunities for structure modelling and detailing. Because the prototype is often cramped, with tracks winding between numerous buildings we can fit a great deal into a small area on a layout without loss of realism. There are a number of fine kits for industrial structures on the market, mainly plastic kits manufactured on the Continent. These can be modified and combined to produce even greater variety or the modeller can scratch-build his structures, perhaps following actual prototypes. Several working models are also available as kits including a dock crane, a gantry crane, an aerial ropeway, gravel loaders and a conveyor belt, and these will add extra activity and interest to the layout. The possibilities for detailing an industrial model railway layout are almost limitless and the modeller might like to illuminate the buildings, perhaps employing fibre optics.

If the opportunity arises to build a larger layout eventually the industrial layout can be incorporated into it forming a factory area which can generate much interesting traffic and shunting activity.

Narrow gauge

Not only are the narrow-gauge prototypes very attractive and appealing but they also have many other features which make them ideal subjects for modelling. The short trains, small locomotives and rolling stock, sharp curves, steep gradients and simple station track plans are all useful to the enthusiast trying to fit a model railway into a small space.

The modeller may choose to base his layout on one of the preserved lines, either as it is today or as it was in its earlier days. There are a number of locomotive and rolling stock kits now available, mainly in 009, for British prototypes which will assist the modeller in a project of this sort but he will also need to do some converting and scratch-building to complete the roster. Obviously if the modeller chooses to represent the line as it is today there will be no problem in gaining accurate information about the railway and its stock. There is also a good deal of data available about the better known railways in their earlier days so it should not be too difficult to make an authentic model.

Alternatively, the enthusiast may prefer to model an imaginary line thus giving him more scope for introducing features he finds interesting or attractive. He may base his model in a general way on one prototype or perhaps on aspects of several.

Railway types

The Vale of Tallynog is a model of a small Welsh narrow-gauge railway constructed by Phil Savage, a member of the Wessex 009 Society. The fiddle yard can be seen behind the retaining wall. The excellent detailing of the railway terminus and dock gives the layout a very realistic appearance.

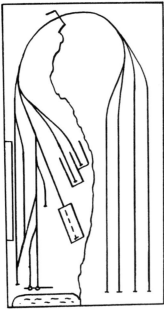

Track plan for Phil Savage's 009 Vale of Tallynog layout, a U-shaped terminus to fiddle yard design. (Plan not to scale.)

Many of the overseas narrow-gauge lines are also very appealing and with the selection of ready-to-run models, particularly Swiss and Austrian prototypes, in HO9 a layout can be built without difficulty. For realism, the modeller should try to create the atmosphere of the original by studying book or magazine pictures and perhaps by visiting the real thing on holiday. The track arrangements differ from those typical of British practice and the model should be based on actual track plans if possible. While the availability of ready-to-run equipment and the greater familiarity of European prototypes tempts modellers to choose these there are many attractive narrow-gauge railways in other parts of the world which could also make excellent layouts. An example is Howard Coulson's 'Eitomo' layout in 009 based on East African prototypes. Study of the real thing from books and magazines together with good scenic work has enabled Howard to capture the atmosphere of these lines very effectively. Most of his locomotives and rolling stock are conversions of commercially available 009 or N-scale models and are closely based on East African prototypes.

Many American narrow-gauge modellers work in HOn3, HO-scale models of 3 ft gauge

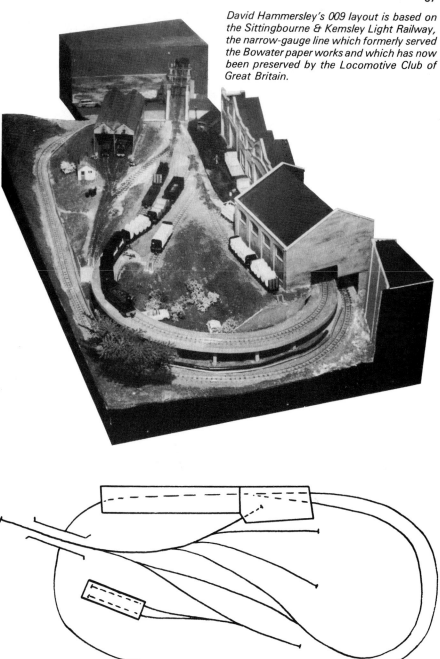

David Hammersley's 009 layout is based on the Sittingbourne & Kemsley Light Railway, the narrow-gauge line which formerly served the Bowater paper works and which has now been preserved by the Locomotive Club of Great Britain.

Track plan of the 009 layout built by David Hammersley and based on the Bowater Railway. The track design is an oval, partly concealed by structures, with a branch rising from it to the higher central part of the layout. (Plan is not to scale.)

Railway types

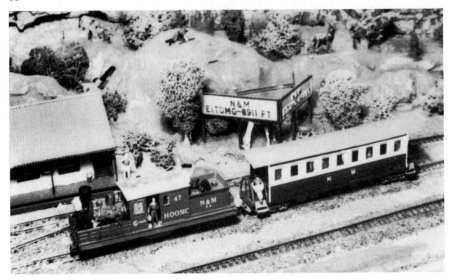

Howard Coulson has based his 009 narrow-gauge 'Eitomo' layout on East African prototype lines. With careful research and imaginative modelling he has given his layout the atmosphere of the real thing. The locomotives (including the Climax shown here) and rolling stock are mostly conversions of commercial 009- and N-scale products.

prototypes, but some are using 9 mm gauge to model lines such as the Maine 2 ft gauge railways in HO scale, and this would be a more convenient choice for modellers in Britain as there are more commercial items available for conversion.

The introduction of ready-to-run models in 009 led to the development of the so-called 'rabbit' layouts. Modellers took advantage of the sharp curves and steep gradients possible in this scale to pack a great deal of track at various levels onto a very small baseboard, with mountainous scenery and with trains popping in and out of tunnels like rabbits in and out of burrows. Realism is of course compromised but the layouts are very entertaining to build and operate. With good scenery they are very attractive and make an ideal coffee table or display layout for the lounge.

An alternative to an entire layout in narrow gauge is the addition of a narrow-gauge feeder to a standard-gauge layout. This is an ideal arrangement as it gives you a chance to see how you like narrow-gauge modelling without committing yourself to more than a short length of track to start with. If you like it you can then extend the narrow-gauge section. I should perhaps warn you that there is a tendency for it to take over at the expense of the standard gauge! A narrow-gauge line will add interest and extra activity to the

layout using only space which would not be of much use for standard-gauge tracks.

Combining standard and narrow gauge on the layout gives the opportunity for including interesting dual-gauge trackwork. However, with the exception of a dual 16.5 mm/9 mm gauge crossing made by Lilliput, you will have to build any dual-gauge track yourself, a task for the more experienced modeller.

Lilliput make this crossing for 00 gauge (16.5 mm) and 009 (9 mm) which may be useful when combining a standard- and narrow-gauge line on a layout.

Foreign

I have made some mention of modelling foreign railways in the section on narrow gauge and similar principles apply to standard gauge with regard to familiarising yourself with everything about the prototype and its setting if you hope to create a realistic

This 009 narrow-gauge layout owned by the Poole & District Model Railway Society measures only 36 in × 27 in but includes a track run of over 12 ft, two sidings, two stations and many interesting scenic features! It is an example of the so-called rabbit layout.

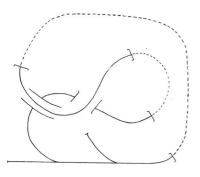

The Poole & District MRS 009 layout is a simple 'rabbit' type with a dog bone design where one loop partly overlaps the other. Two sidings add extra interest. (Plan not to scale.)

model. Operating practice and track layout is often rather different from the British system and this should be taken into account when designing a layout.

For US modelling the range of ready-to-run models, kits and parts in HO and N scales is excellent and the enthusiast can obtain a great deal of information about modelling American railroads from reading one or more of the excellent model railroad magazines produced in the States.

The range of European models in HO and N scales is also very good though the emphasis is almost entirely on ready-to-run equipment; this is generally of excellent quality. Some countries, particularly Germany, France and Switzerland, are very well catered for by the manufacturers but for others there is much less available. There is a good deal of prototype information, in England, for the modeller and several countries have model railway magazines, though here there may be language problems of course. Ideally one should visit the country concerned and take as many photographs as possible to guide you in modelling the setting, the trackside details and so on.

For other countries of the world much converting or scratch-building will be required to complete a layout and such a project is only suitable for the more experienced modeller with a particular interest in and knowledge of the railway system concerned.

Preserved line

I briefly mentioned the possibility of modelling a preserved line in the narrow-gauge section. For the modeller who likes, and has perhaps already collected, a wide variety of locomotives which would not normally be seen together because of their origins, period or type, a very attractive solution can be a preserved standard-gauge line. One could even include some foreign

A scene on a typical US branchline modelled in HO scale. The beautifully detailed corrugated iron warehouse was built from a Campbell's kit. (Photograph by courtesy of Leo Campbell.)

Jouef offer a wide selection of French prototype models in HO scale including this interesting train of double-decker commuter coaches seen here on the Hestair Models' exhibition layout.

engines if desired as there are several prototype precedents for this!

The modeller might like to base his layout on an actual preserved line. This has the advantage that he can visit the railway to see and photograph everything and there is often plenty of published data about the locomotives, rolling stock and so on. The model could be a representation of the line as it is, or as the preservation society hope to make it. Such a model could be very satisfying and could also have considerable publicity value for the railway. Providing locomotives and stock for most lines should not be a problem using the standard commercial products.

Another approach would be to model a branch line you like and which has been closed, as though it had been preserved. This will give you more freedom in the design of the layout and in the choice of locomotives

and rolling stock than if you were modelling an actual preserved line. A third alternative is to model an entirely imaginary preserved line of your own design.

There are many interesting details which could be added to a layout of this type. There may be locomotives and stock awaiting or undergoing repair, some scrapped items kept to provide spare parts for other stock, many parts lying around, and numerous visitors, some with cameras taking pictures. There could also be a small museum of other items such as traction engines, vintage cars or buses, and so on.

If you model a station on the preserved line as one combined with British Rail then you have the perfect excuse for including everything from vintage steam engines on the preserved line to the High Speed Train on the BR tracks! All on the one layout!

The working traverser on Mike Sharman's period layout with its nicely detailed vertical boilered donkey engine. The locomotive is 'Pegasus' a 2-4-0 built in 1870 by Joseph Beattie for the London & South Western Railway. Locomotive and traverser were both hand-built.

More specialised railway types

Engine depot

One approach to modelling on a small layout is to choose a prototype line which can be compressed without losing its essential features, the branch line being a good example. Another method can be to select a small part of a larger prototype system and model only that section. As many modellers buy or build more and larger locomotives than can reasonably be accommodated on the usual small layout, an apt choice can be to model a motive power depot. Such a model need occupy only a small area but will be ideal as a setting for displaying and operating locomotive models. If hidden sidings are included the layout could even be

Part of the garden railway layout built by Dave Howsam and Ron Prattley. Figures, plants and garden fittings are Britains' models. (Photo by Ron Prattley.)

operated to a timetable, with locomotives leaving the shed, taking on coal and water and proceeding to their duties. Later they will return from the hidden sidings to be prepared for the next day's work.

Though such a layout is unusual it could be interesting to build, with plenty of opportunities for super-detailing interesting structures and, if desired, a turntable. A crane and a snowplough are among the items of unusual rolling stock which can be stored on sidings on the layout. Extra details could include a hoist and perhaps an engine undergoing repairs, or one which has been scrapped. The scope of the model can be increased by providing facilities for diesels as well.

A layout of this type could be ideal for the modeller who is a club member and can enjoy more conventional operating on the club layout but wants somewhere to display his locomotives. It is also a useful unit for the modeller who has no space for a layout at present but is building up a collection of locomotive models for the time when he will be able to construct a layout. The engine depot will allow him to enjoy some construction work, provide a setting for his engines and can be incorporated into a layout later.

Military railways

From the American Civil War right through to the Second World War, railways have played an important military role. With the great popularity of both railway and military modelling I am sure that many enthusiasts are interested in both and I am surprised that so few military railway layouts have been built. The ideal prototype would perhaps be the extensive narrow-gauge railway system which operated in France during the First World War tanks, soldiers and horse-drawn *First World War* by W.J.K. Davies (David & Charles) covers this subject in detail, even including dimensioned drawings of the locomotives and rolling stock. In 009 the equipment could be represented well with commercially available items, modified in some cases. Such a layout could be built in a small space and the scenic work could be very effective, with ruined buildings, First World War tanks, soldiers and horse drawn equipment, trenches, look-out posts and so on. The Airfix 00-scale military models would be especially useful in this detailing.

Some of the most interesting and impressive pieces of military railway equipment are the railway guns, and the enthusiast may well like to include several of these models on his layout. One approach might be to construct an industrial railway layout based on a factory producing these guns. Such a model would permit shunting and also act as an effective setting for displaying the model rail guns.

A different type of military railway layout would be one based on one of the military railways operated in Britain. The Longmoor Military Railway used for training army personnel in railway operating has been well documented and could make an interesting model. The Royal Aircraft Establishment railway at Farnborough would make an unusual variant on the industrial railway theme. The major traffic here is coal brought in by rail to the power station, but wood and steel sections are also transported.

Rack railways

Mountain railways may be fitted with a rack in the centre of the track with which a driven gear on the locomotives meshes thus ensuring good traction and no slipping. The only British prototype is the Snowdon Mountain Railway.

In model form Fleischmann provide locomotives and track, but no points, for both HO and N scales. The lack of points mean that only a simple single track line can be constructed unless the modeller is prepared to make points himself. However, a rack railway can be an attractive addition to a conventional layout, providing extra activity and an excuse for some mountainous scenery.

Underground railways

Underground railways have been rather neglected by modellers though there does seem to have been more interest recently with the appearance of a few layouts including models of London Transport tube trains, one built by an enthusiast in Holland! An LT layout would make an interesting model. Much of the track should be modelled on parts of the system above ground with only part of it in tunnels. Alternatively, an underground model could be added to an ordinary urban or suburban area layout, in which case it might be best to keep it entirely beneath ground level so that it does not take up space which could be used for the rest of the layout.

Garden railway

Dave Howsam and Ron Prattley produced a most unusual but attractive model some years ago of a garden in 10 mm to the foot scale using Britains' figures and garden fittings with N-scale model locomotives,

More specialised railway types

The relatively small size of N-scale models has enabled Graham Bailey to provide comprehensive steam and diesel locomotive servicing facilities on his moderate sized British Rail layout. These include a steam locomotive roundhouse (above left), coaling stage (above), diesel engine house (left), diesel fuelling depot (below left) and a train washing unit (below).

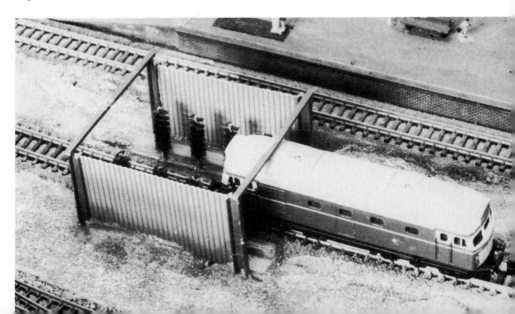

A model tramway system can be an interesting addition to a model railway layout. The two views above and right are of Adrian Swain's 00-scale tramway. British tram models are available in 00 and N scales as cast metal kits; Continental prototype models are manufactured as ready-to-run items in HO and N scales.

rolling stock and track representing a 10 ¼ in gauge garden railway. The track layout on this model was very simple so operating scope was limited but the layout was intended especially for display and was very successful. There is no reason why a more extensive system could not be modelled in this way. A miniature railway, though not of course in the garden, which would make a very interesting prototype for a project of this sort is the well known Ravenglass & Eskdale Railway.

Monorails

These make intriguing models but do call for scratch-building by the modeller. Though model monorails are rather rare, the Listowel & Ballybunion (an early Irish monorail) seems to be an appealing prototype, perhaps because it is so unusual. I know of models of this line in various scales by no fewer than five modellers; the largest of these models are the superb 16 mm scale locomotives made by Don Boreham and Adrian Garner.

Trams

Trams are not strictly railway models in the usual sense, though a tramway layout can be very appealing. The sharp curves and short 'trains' (for British prototypes usually a single

tramcar, though European trams often pull trailers) enable an interesting layout to be built in a small area. As the setting will probably be an urban one the possibilities for structure modelling and detailing are considerable. A tram system can also be added to a model railway layout and will increase the action on the layout, even with a very simple tram system.

Ready-to-run European tram models are available in HO and N scales while British cast metal kits are made in 00 and N scales. A few HO-scale German prototype cast metal tram kits are also produced.

Most modellers will want to build a conventional type of layout, the branch line and industrial railway being particularly suitable for the beginner. However, I feel it is worth while to indicate, as I have above, that the possible scope in the hobby is much wider than that; it is always worth while considering something a little different for your modelling, provided it is a subject which appeals to you and in which you are sufficiently interested to do any research which is necessary.

More specialised railway types

Track planning

00 scale

Having looked at the basic track schemes and considered the various types of railways that can be modelled we have reached the stage of planning the track arrangement for a layout. The usual method is to draw to scale the outline of the layout baseboard and then to plot in the tracks on this plan. A convenient scale is 1 in to the foot or, for small layouts, even 2 in to the foot. Unfortunately many plans are not drawn properly, either through lack of care or due to a desire to squeeze that little bit more into the layout. The errors particularly relate to points, for which inadequate allowance is made for lengths and radii, and to clearances which are insufficient. It is very important to draw everything accurately to scale as errors here will cause problems later when you try to construct the layout. Though a neatly drawn out plan (complete with attractive scenic details sketched in) looks very nice it is by no means necessary for this planning work. A roughly drawn plan is perfectly adequate provided the modeller keeps accurately to scale measurements.

Tracks should be arranged so that the centre lines are not less than 1 ½ in from the baseboard edge and a greater clearance is better if it is possible. The track centres for 2 tracks running parallel should be 2 in apart. The curve radius chosen as the minimum will depend on the type of equipment that will be run on the layout, on the space available and on the type of railway modelled. The usual minimum for proprietary models is 15 in radius, but 18 or 24 in curves are desirable, and curves of larger radius still will look better if they can be accommodated. When plotting the track positions we must start a curve at a point a distance at least equal to the radius of the curve plus the clearance needed, from the end of the layout. If the curve can be started further back we can either use a larger radius curve or allow more clearance. As the curve is often one of 180° at the end of the layout we must also check on the width,

which will be twice the sum of the radius and the clearance, in relation to the baseboard width. The appearance of small radius curves can be improved considerably by fitting a curve of twice the radius between the straight and the true curve as a transitional section. This will require more space than the simple minimum radius curve, of course, and suitable allowance must be made if you wish to do this.

Points are more difficult to draw to scale and care should be taken to allow sufficient space for them. You should measure the points you intend to use and use this length as a guide, preferably allowing a little extra to give you some leeway in case of any slight errors during track laying. For example, I allow 7 in for Hornby, 8 in for Peco 2 ft radius, and 9 in for Peco 3 ft radius points, and 8 in for a Peco crossing. I want to stress that you should stick closely to the measurements for points and crossings and resist any temptation to cut things finer. These parts cannot be altered so if you have not allowed the right amount of space your layout will not be correct — other parts being distorted with detrimental effects.

A fairly commonly employed track arrangement is a reversing loop. This requires a distance of three times the radius of the curves for the loop itself, together with another radius on the end to join with the other tracks. The width of the loop is twice the radius. Clearances must be added to these figures.

If one track is to pass over another a clearance of at least 2 ½ in and preferably 3 in is required. As the maximum gradient that should be used is 1 in 30 a distance of 90 in, 7 ft 6 in, is needed to clear the low level track if only one track is on a gradient. If one track rises and the other falls, both at 1 in 30, the distance is halved to 45 in, 3 ft 9 in respectively. These figures assume the more desirable minimum of 3 in clearance is adopted. If the track is curved we need to

Diagram A

Diagram B

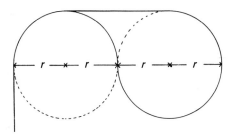

Track planning in 00 scale *Many modellers when drawing out a scale plan make the points too short and give them too wide an angle; this causes problems when you try to construct the layout as the points will not fit into the space allowed.*

If we draw in the centre lines for the straight and diverging tracks on a pair of points as in Diagram A we can see there is a point at which these lines meet and that they meet at an angle. To draw points accurately on our track plans we need to locate the point at which the lines meet correctly and to draw the true angle from it.

We can do this as in Diagram B, using the dimensions given in the table for 'A' and 'B', and we can then be confident that the plan will be accurate with respect to the points.

Point radius	'A'	'B'
18 inch	*2½ inch*	*3½ units*
24 inch	*3 inch*	*4 units*
36 inch	*3½ inch*	*5 units*

These dimensions are easily obtained by measuring directly the points you intend to use and you can make your own listing to suit your choice of points.

![reversing loop diagram with two circles and a dashed curve, labelled r across the base]

The reversing loop together with a lead out is equivalent in space to two circles side by side and the length required is therefore at least four times the minimum radius.

know its length for working out the gradient. As the circumference of a circle is given by $2\pi r$ we will be close enough if we call π 3 and reckon the circumference as 6 times the radius. That is in every ¼ circle the track distance is 1½ times the radius. For 18 in radius curves therefore, the distance for a quarter circle is 27 in.

Station platforms will be 4½-5 in wide and the platform edge should be an inch from the track centre line. Platform lengths depend on the train lengths and a convenient estimate is to allow 1 ft per coach. If platforms must be short, model a small station and keep train lengths down also. Stations are usually modelled with straight platforms but the introduction of a slight curve can be attractive.

A terminus station will need a run-around loop so that the engine can be moved to the other end of the train for the return journey. The loop can either go alongside the platform or can be on the line beyond the platform so it may also be used for goods trains. The loop must, of course, be long enough to hold the trains and there must also be sufficient room on the track beyond it for the locomotive, say 8 in for a tank engine and as much as 12 in for a tender locomotive.

Goods facilities can be very simple, merely a siding or two entered by trailing points, or there may be a larger yard with a headshunt, so that shunting can take place without blocking the main line. A run-around loop may be provided but often the passenger loop can be shared. When planning sidings and passing loops try to avoid reverse or 'S' curves.

Kick-back sidings are sometimes included on a model railway layout. Access to one of these is only possible if the siding from which it leads is empty already or is cleared at the time. Because of this the modeller may find that he does not use the kick-back siding as he does not want to be bothered with carrying out the extra moves required. Conversely, however, we can take the view that anything which involves more shunting movements adds to the operating activity and makes the layout more interesting. It is a matter of personal choice whether you want to keep operation simple and easy or to make it as complex as you can. Modellers who particularly enjoy operation and shunting may choose to model an industrial line on which numerous complications such as kick-back sidings, several industries being served by one siding making access more difficult, and so on, can be introduced.

Engine servicing facilities may also be very

Track planning

Some examples of station plans — not to scale.

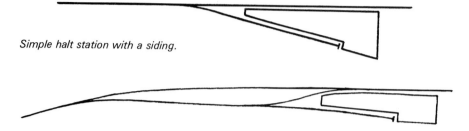

Simple halt station with a siding.

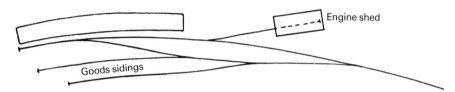

Simple through station with run around loop so trains from either direction can shunt the siding and so trains can be reversed. The loop can also double up as a siding.

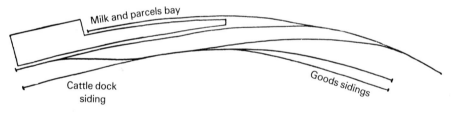

Engine shed

Goods sidings

Small terminus station with run-around loop, goods sidings and engine shed.

Milk and parcels bay

Cattle dock siding

Goods sidings

Slightly larger terminus station with parcels, milk and cattle dock sidings but no engine shed.

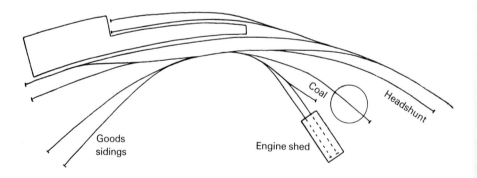

Coal

Headshunt

Goods sidings

Engine shed

Larger terminus station with more comprehensive engine servicing facilities including a turntable so tender locomotives can be turned. A headshunt has been provided so shunting can be carried out without blocking the main line.

Model Railway Guide 2

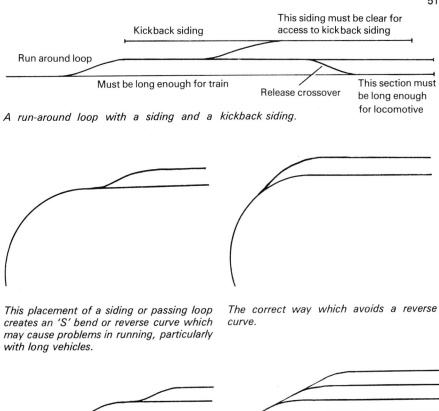

Kickback siding

This siding must be clear for access to kickback siding

Run around loop

Must be long enough for train

Release crossover

This section must be long enough for locomotive

A run-around loop with a siding and a kickback siding.

This placement of a siding or passing loop creates an 'S' bend or reverse curve which may cause problems in running, particularly with long vehicles.

The correct way which avoids a reverse curve.

This arrangement of sidings creates a whole series of reverse curves and also wastes space.

The correct design for a series of sidings.

simple, merely a single track engine shed with coaling stage, water tower and ash pit for one engine at a branch line terminus, or a larger depot may be modelled with a 2 or 3 track shed and perhaps a turntable for tender locomotives. If a point-to-point system has a turntable at one terminus there should also be one at the other terminus (except, of course, if it is a fiddle yard) so that engines can always run facing the correct way. A turntable is quite a large feature so you should consider carefully before including one if you are short of space. A 9 in diameter table will accommodate small engines but larger locomotives will need an 11 in table.

It is essential to provide proper access to track, points and rolling stock; check your own easy reach at the height you intend to have your layout and use this as a guide when planning the layout. If you want to have a

central operating well do not make this too small; 4 ft × 2ft is a reasonable minimum. Make sure that access to tunnels will also be easy.

For the actual drawing out only fairly simple drawing instruments are needed; a sharp pencil, a pair of compasses, a set square, a ruler and an eraser are the essentials. Templates, for the curves you will be using in the scale of your drawing, can be cut from card or, even better, transparent plastic, and will be very useful. Many modellers work on white card rather than on paper when drawing up layout plans as frequent alterations can be made without crumpling the material or spoiling the surface.

While it is very convenient to draw out plans to 1 or 2 in to the foot scale in the early stages, there is much to be said for drawing

Track planning

Small motive power depots.

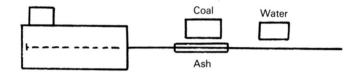

Very simple engine facilities for a small station.

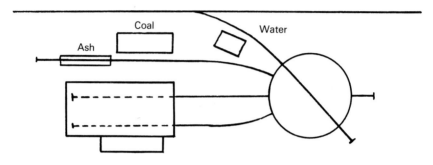

Larger dead-end type of shed with turntable.

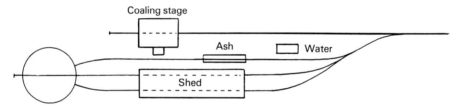

Through type of engine shed with turntable.

out your plan full size when you have reached what you think may be your final design. Lining paper used for wall-papering is cheap and convenient for this purpose. You will need a long ruler, a pencil, an eraser, and some templates for the radii you will be using — cut from card, hardboard or ply. It is usually most convenient to work on the floor. If you are planning to use Peco points you will find a set of the Peco point plans valuable. By working full size you can avoid errors that can easily arise in small scale plans.

N scale

In general the principles of planning in N scale are similar to those for 00 scale with an appropriate reduction in dimensions, but there are a few special points to bear in mind. As the majority of published track plans are designed for 00 or HO scale it may well be that the modeller will wish to adapt such a

plan for N scale. As a rough guide we can halve the linear dimensions reducing the area to a quarter. However, a direct conversion in this way may be neither possible nor desirable. The size of the operator is, of course, the same no matter what the scale of the layout, thus if there is a central operating well or some access openings it will probably be impossible to reduce the size of these. However, as the overall dimensions will be greatly reduced, while the operator's reach remains the same, the whole of the layout may now be accessible from any of the edges allowing the modeller to operate from one side instead of from the central well, which can then be covered with scenery. If a central well is retained the layout size cannot be reduced as much but if you have enough space it is worth while keeping the well. The layout will appear more realistic if viewed and operated from the centre as only part will be visible at any one time making the round and round nature of the line, if a continuous run design, much less apparent.

It is often undesirable to reduce an 00-scale plan to quarter size for N scale; the resulting appearance is likely to be very disappointing with a much more toy-like effect than if it had been built in the larger scale. This is because the actual size of the layout is so much smaller and the eye sees so much more of it at a single glance. This is aggravated by the fact that the viewing position remains the same height above the layout, and is now twice as high in proportion. If you measure out a 6 ft × 4 ft rectangle and a 3 ft × 2 ft rectangle and compare them you will get some idea of this effect. If there is an oval, its continuous design is more obvious than in the original size. Things can be improved a little by building the layout higher from the ground so that you do not look down on it as much, but if possible it is better to reduce the linear dimensions only to about three-quarters of the 00 size rather than to half. This will allow the use of larger radius curves and give a generally less cramped appearance.

Another point which must be considered is the clearance for raised tracks crossing over low level tracks beneath. As the track base thickness will probably be the same as for 00 scale and as the same or greater clearance in actual terms will be required, the clearances cannot be reduced proportionally with the other dimensions. This will mean that an increase in the gradient will be needed for the N-scale layout. This is another reason for

reducing the layout size by less than the full half.

If you have a larger space available but are thinking of N scale rather than 00 to allow you to build a more extensive and interesting model railway it is essential not to be too ambitious. We have become used to thinking of an 00-scale layout of say 8 ft × 4 ft as being within the capabilities of a beginner and it may be tempting to think of an N-scale layout in the same area. If the track plan is kept simple with not too many points, and emphasis is more on sweeping curves, gentle gradients and realistic landscape, this may be very successful. However, it is likely to be disastrous if an attempt is made to use the space for an N-scale version of a complex 16 ft × 8 ft 00-scale layout designed for a group of advanced modellers! This may be an exaggeration but it is very easy to get carried away with enthusiasm in the circumstances and some restraint is needed.

The fact that a 180° turn can be made in N scale (in as little as 20 in of baseboard width) creates some possibilities not open to the modeller working in 00 scale. For example, on a branch line terminus to fiddle yard scheme it is possible in N scale to include a reversing loop with some hidden sidings arising from it in place of the usual fiddle yard, making operation more convenient. Similarly, loops can be fitted at each end of a long, narrow layout to make it a continuous run design without making the layout too wide to be fitted along a wall or two walls of a room.

Eight Oaks station on a British N (1:48) scale layout built by Bob Jones. In N scale, platforms long enough to look realistic can be provided without needing a large space.

Track planning

Structures

The structures on a model railway layout are a very important part of the landscape. Not only do they add scenic interest but in some cases they also provide extra operational possibilities for the line by creating traffic. For the best effect, both for individual buildings and for the overall appearance of the layout some planning in the selection and positioning is essential. Any temptation to just rush out to the local model shop once the track is down and to buy whatever takes the eye, or happens to be in stock at the time, is to be resisted!

In some cases a structure model needs to be planned accurately at an early stage. For example, the beautifully modelled machine shop on Mike Sharman's period layout is an integral part of the layout design so its size and position, and the position of the tracks, standard, narrow and broad gauge, entering it all had to be decided before the track laying was carried out. In other situations it may be important to plan ahead to ensure that there will be sufficient space for a particular model building, and that the sidings will be suitably positioned in relation to it. This will give a more realistic result than merely making the structures fit in later with the tracks already in place. The dimensions of model buildings constructed from the kits of some manufacturers are listed in their catalogues and this can be useful in advance planning.

We can divide model railway structures into three main groups, the railway buildings, such as stations, goods sheds, engine sheds and so on; buildings associated with the railway and providing traffic for it, factories, mines, warehouses, etc and incidental buildings in the landscape, houses, farms, hotels, garages, shops, and so on.

There is a good range of model buildings, mostly in kit form, available commercially in 00/HO and N scales, and these can often be easily modified or converted to suit your requirements more closely and to give you some individuality for your layout. Another popular technique is the combination of parts from two or more kits, known as cross-kitting, to make larger or different structures.

The greatest choice and scope, of course, comes with scratch-building structures for your layout. A good selection of materials is stocked by model shops including brick, stone and tile papers, balsa, plastic and corrugated copper.

Whether you use kits or construct your own buildings from scratch you should choose prototypes appropriate to the locality in which your railway is supposed to be set and to the type of railway you are modelling. The architectural style and details and the construction material used—wood, brick or stone—are often characteristic and the right selection can do much to make your layout appear authentic.

Most of us have space for only a small layout and beginners should start modestly even if there is plenty of room available, hence there is space for only relatively few buildings so we should be quite selective. Each should be worth its place on the layout and must add to the interest and overall appearance. We need buildings with character which will fit in with each other and generally they should be fairly small as large structures may tend to dwarf the rest of the layout. Buildings with interesting or irregular lines, with varying textures due to the use of several different materials such as brick, stone, wood, corrugated iron, and with additions, alterations and repairs over the years, together with the effects of weathering, often make good modelling subjects. Generally I find the older buildings more attractive in model form than the new modern structures. Remember that on a layout the view point is almost always from above and roofs are particularly noticeable. Thus buildings with varied rooflines due to gables and dormers, and with interesting chimneys and other roof details are especially suitable for modelling purposes.

Just as important as the selection of which structures will make good individual models

These low relief warehouses at the rear of the industrial layout built by Allan Sibley and Brian Dorman complete the scene and also conceal a fiddle yard.

This superbly detailed railway workshop on Mike Sharman's period layout is an important feature of the railway. Note the three different track gauges inside the building with, from the front, broad-, narrow- and standard-gauge tracks.

is the choice and arrangement to form a visually effective grouping. This takes a bit of practice and experience but can make all the difference in the final appearance. Develop a sense of arrangement by studying groupings which you find visually appealing—both in pictures of prototype structures and of layouts built by the expert scenic modellers and shown in the model press—and try to decide why they look good. Experiment with separate models, putting them in various positions in relation to one another until you find the best arrangement. You will soon learn how to achieve a good effect on your layout. In general avoid very regular patterns with straight streets and buildings in orderly

Structures

The arrangement of the structures in this attractive 00-scale display layout featuring Builder Plus kits has been planned to create a realistic model town and the railway blends naturally into the scene.

rows. More irregular arrangements are not only more typical of the prototype but will also make your layout appear larger.

A very effective technique where space is limited at the rear of a layout is the use of low relief structures. These are buildings with only the front wall and the front parts of the side walls and roof modelled while the rest is omitted. Although the models have a depth of only an inch or so they look correct from any viewing angle provided that other buildings, trees or other features are placed to conceal the lack of depth. The appearance is much more realistic than merely using a painted backscene. Some special kits are available for structures of this type, for example, the card kits made by Superquick and Hamblings, or alternatively you can use ordinary kits and employ the front and back separately as low relief models. If you prefer to scratch-build these models they are, of course, much quicker and easier to construct than conventional structures as only the front is fully modelled.

Structure models can also be utilised as scenic barriers to visually break up a length of track to make it appear longer, or to conceal part of an oval of track or a fiddle yard. Low relief structures near the back of the layout are especially useful in covering hidden tracks, storage sidings or a fiddle yard. A row of buildings along the centre of the baseboard, with or without a double-sided backdrop, can divide the layout into two separate towns making the railway seem longer and the stations further away from each other.

There are a number of kits available now for structures which are motorised. These include windmills with moving sails, water-mills fitted with small pumps so that real water can be circulated to turn the wheels, factories with moving conveyor belts and so on. Though some modellers may feel that these are rather gimmicky they are well worth considering, particularly on a small layout where any extra movement which can be introduced, in addition to the trains, will add to the interest of the scene. There are also some excellent working crane models for dock and goods yard use.

You may like to include on your layout two linked industries, between which there is rail traffic — for example, a mine from which ore is taken to a processing plant. For the most realistic effect the wagons in trains from the mine should be loaded with ore, while trains of empty wagons run back from the processing plant to the mine. To avoid the task of loading and unloading by hand many modellers ignore the inaccuracy and run full and empty wagons indiscriminately. However, a neat scheme to allow correct running

Many excellent industrial structures are available in kit form so it is easy to provide an interesting variety for a layout. Although the Continental kits are in HO or Continental N scale they can be used satisfactorily for 00- and British N-scale layouts respectively. This well detailed model is the Kibri HO-scale Large Gravel Silo.

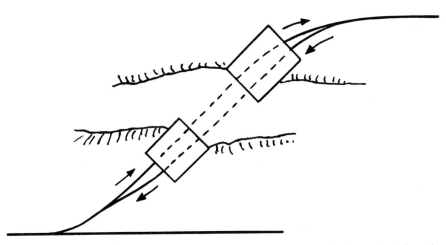

This arrangement allows empty wagons to enter the mine and full ones to leave it, while at the processing plant the reverse occurs, without the need for any loading or unloading of wagons.

has been devised by some modellers. The two industries are positioned either side of a ridge of hills, a row of industrial buildings or a double sided backdrop and hidden tracks connect them as shown in the diagram. Thus full wagons pushed into the processing plant are removed from the mine (and conversely empty wagons pushed into the mine are pulled out) at the other end of the hidden track from the processing plant.

Structures

Scenery

There is often a tendency for the modeller to concentrate on the designing of a track plan which will provide interesting operation, on the laying of smooth track for good running and on the correct wiring of the track. Once satisfied with these aspects he then adds scenery very much as an afterthought. Unfortunately such scenic work often appears unnatural and contrived. This is a pity because scenery can do a great deal to make a layout more realistic and interesting. Good scenic work not only makes the layout more attractive but also makes it look larger than it actually is. The scenery can also help to disguise such operationally necessary features as sharp curves, hidden tracks and fiddle yards. It can also be used to emphasise features we wish to show up.

It is important to plan the scenery in a general way with the track plan. Do not worry about the smaller details at this stage, as there will almost certainly be minor changes you wish to make during construction. In the prototype the landscape is, obviously, there before the railway which is planned to run through it. In the model the scenery is added last, but we should try to make it look as if it were there first. We must consider the type of terrain we want to model (hilly or flat, rural or urban) and the placing of a river, lake or canal. If your model is to be set in a particular location it is worth while visiting the area to see what the landscape is like. Make sketches or take photographs to guide you later when you are working on your layout.

By building up the scenery in the central part of this small 00-scale layout Terry Jenkins has created a dividing barrier between the two sides of the layout helping to conceal the oval track plan and making the layout more realistic.

Wherever there are tracks hidden by scenery, adequate access must be provided for track maintenance and in case of stalling or derailment. This is particularly important if there are concealed points or crossings. On the Isle of Purbeck MRC the problem has been solved by making part of the scenery lift out to give access to the track and points inside a tunnel. The removable section includes the farm.

Scenery

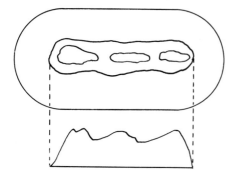

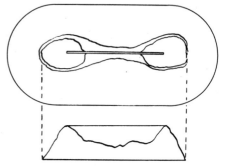

Scenery can be used to separate visually the two sides of an oval to make the layout appear larger and more interesting. A ridge of hills can be modelled to form a scenic barrier.

Extra height can be given by modelling a peak at each end of the ridge and fitting a double-sided backdrop between.

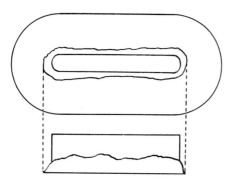

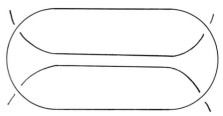

If the modelled scenery cannot be made high enough, an oval backscene can be erected within the track oval. This continuous backdrop will be more realistic than a simple, flat, double-sided backscene in which the ends would be visible.

Taking the idea of a scenic barrier even further, the two sides of the track oval can be completely separated visually with backscenes as shown and the scenery can be quite different on each side. If a station is provided at each side this set-up is a good one for two operators, one at each side of the layout.

In scenic modelling considerable compression is needed and we must choose small examples of natural features, hills, rivers, trees and so on for modelling because otherwise they will be too big for the layout. It is better to select a narrow, winding river rather than a wide, straight one because the former will appear longer making the layout look larger. Another useful technique is to model a number of separate scenes, each one forming a centre of interest to attract the attention of the viewer, within the layout as a whole. Breaking the layout up into a number of parts like this makes it seem bigger. In the same way visually breaking lengths of tracks up into sections by bridges, cuttings, tunnels and buildings will also make them appear longer.

Tunnels are very useful on a model railway for hiding tracks, for example, to conceal part of the continuous run of an oval track plan and as a scenic break. However, real tunnels are very expensive for railways to bore so they are only constructed where they are really needed. Thus for a convincing appearance on a model railway the hill through which the tunnel passes must look high and large enough so that it would not have been possible to carry the track around the hill or through a cutting. If the model is set in a generally flat landscape it may be preferable to use some other scenic feature such as a group of trees, a road bridge or a structure to act as a scenic barrier, rather than to introduce an unlikely hill and tunnel. If you have one or more tunnels on your layout make sure that the clearances inside the tunnels are adequate for your widest models and that access is provided for maintenance of track, and points (if any) and for retrieving trains which have stalled or derailed within the tunnels.

On an oval plan layout a useful scenic arrangement is a high central ridge of hills. This device divides the layout into two areas viewed separately and makes the layout appear larger and the length of run seem longer. It also means that as there is a barrier the two areas can be made quite different scenically, adding variety to the model. If the ridge cannot be high enough to give visual separation without being unrealistically steep, some trees can be added along the top. If the scenery in the centre cannot be built up high enough, an alternative is to use a double-sided backdrop, either between a peak at each end or as an oval (see diagrams).

Scenic backgrounds fitted to the rear of a layout can do a great deal to improve the appearance by blocking from view irrelevant and distracting features such as wall-paper, curtains and so on, behind the layout and by making the layout appear larger by giving the impression that it extends into the distance as far as the eye can see. A scenic background can also be useful in concealing tracks or a fiddle yard.

For the most realistic effect it is important to match the modelled scenery and the background so that they appear to merge imperceptibly. This requires some advance planning particularly if a commercially produced backscene is employed as the modelled scenery must then be designed to blend into this.

Well modelled suburban scenery adds interest to this scene on a Fleischmann exhibition layout in HO scale. Study of such model railways can provide many ideas for scenic work on small home layouts.

A model of the layout

It is often difficult, particularly for the beginner, to visualise from a small scale layout plan just what the completed model railway will look like. This is especially so when the layout will have track at various levels. One way of deciding if you want to build from a particular plan is to make a small model of the layout at perhaps 1 in to the foot scale. A layout 6 ft × 4 ft would thus be modelled as a 6 in × 4 in miniature. Construction is easy in card and balsa, starting with the lowest level and adding any elevated tracks with card. The terrain can be modelled

with plaster, or a modelling clay such as Das and, if desired, structures and even trains can be added using small pieces of balsa. You can keep such a model very simple using it only to give a rough guide to the appearance of the projected layout or you can add detail and colour to produce a more accurate model. Modifications to the plan can be made easily if desired and you can check that there will be no problems in making such changes. This can save you a lot of time and work later when you come to construct the full size layout.

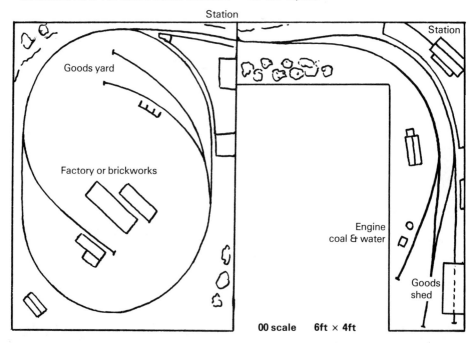

Layout plans *This layout can be developed very simply from a train set. First the oval is laid on a 4 ft × 3 ft baseboard and sidings are added as desired. Finally the extension can be constructed. The design is based on train set track using Hornby or Airfix points. Operation is limited but the layout should be interesting for the beginner to build and run. The layout also provides a good introduction to structure and scenery modelling.*

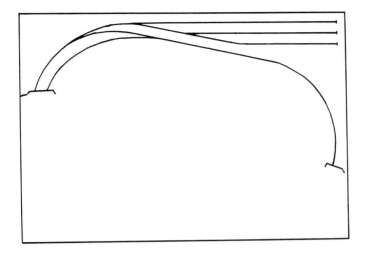

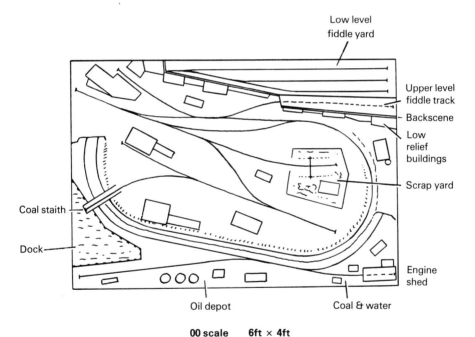

Low level
fiddle yard

Upper level
fiddle track

Backscene

Low
relief
buildings

Scrap yard

Coal staith

Dock

Engine
shed

Oil depot

Coal & water

00 scale   6ft × 4ft

This industrial layout is also a development of the basic oval and again uses Hornby or Airfix points (one Hornby curved point is employed). The low level tracks are laid first and the layout can be operated at this stage. Later the modeller can construct the upper level and the track leading up to it. There is great scope for structure modelling and for scenic detailing and the operating potential is also good if you enjoy shunting. Trains of wagons are brought from the hidden sidings at the rear of the oval and up to the high level where the wagons are distributed to various industries including a scrap yard and a coal staith which passes above the low level tracks to load barges at the dock. Use of one of the card order schemes for deciding which wagon must go to which siding will add to the operating interest. The traffic will be mainly goods but you can also run an occasional workmen's train.

A model of the layout

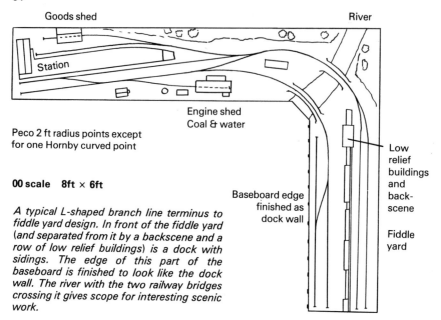

Goods shed   River

Station

Engine shed
Coal & water

Peco 2 ft radius points except
for one Hornby curved point

00 scale   8ft × 6ft

*A typical L-shaped branch line terminus to
fiddle yard design. In front of the fiddle yard
(and separated from it by a backscene and a
row of low relief buildings) is a dock with
sidings. The edge of this part of the
baseboard is finished to look like the dock
wall. The river with the two railway bridges
crossing it gives scope for interesting scenic
work.*

Baseboard edge
finished as
dock wall

Low
relief
buildings
and
back-
scene

Fiddle
yard

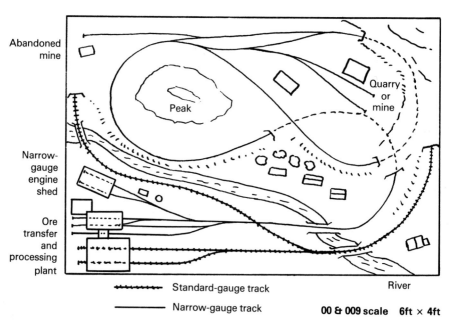

Abandoned
mine

Peak

Quarry
or
mine

Narrow-
gauge
engine
shed

Ore
transfer
and
processing
plant

⊢•••••⊣   Standard-gauge track

──────   Narrow-gauge track   River

00 & 009 scale   6ft × 4ft

*A simple dual-gauge 00/009 layout. The standard-gauge oval with sidings can be laid first and
the layout can be operated in this form until the modeller wishes to add the narrow gauge. The
hidden standard-gauge tracks have been omitted from the plan for clarity, they merely
complete the oval though hidden sidings can also be included if desired. The narrow gauge is
an out and back design and the reversing loop requires special wiring. The dual-gauge
crossing is a Lilliput product. The standard-gauge points are Hornby or Airfix.*

Model Railway Guide 2